Fellow. M. Low ay
Clinton. Va
Aug. 85

gift from The 'Cutler

SMART BARGAINING

SMART BARGAINING
Doing Business with the Japanese

JOHN L. GRAHAM
YOSHIHIRO SANO

BALLINGER PUBLISHING COMPANY
Cambridge, Massachusetts
A Subsidiary of Harper & Row, Publishers, Inc.

International Standard Book Number: 0-88410-729-9

Library of Congress Catalog Card Number: 84-404

Printed in the United States of America

Library of Congress Cataloging in Publication Data

Graham, John L.
    Smart bargaining.

    Includes bibliographical references and index.
    1. Negotiation in business—United States. 2. Negotiation in business—Japan. 3. United States—Commerce—Japan. 4. Japan—Commerce—United States. I. Sano, Yoshihiro. II. Title.
    HD58.6.G7 1984   658.4   84-404
    ISBN 0-88410-729-9

CONTENTS

v

LIST OF FIGURES AND TABLES

LIST OF EXHIBITS

FOREWORD

While associate dean of the business school and director of the International Business Education and Research (IBEAR) program at the University of Southern California, I had the good fortune to work with John Graham and Yoshi Sano. Their book has brought to fruition some of the basic goals we established more than six years ago. In particular, the book is an important step toward bridging cultural differences and thereby reducing transaction costs of business relationships between the two largest economies of the free world: Japan and the United States. Executives of any company having present or future interests in Japan must read and follow the recommendations presented here.

Aside from Canada, our trade relationship with Japan is by far our most important. Some might argue it is the most important given the increasing size of our continuing bilateral trade deficit. Our total merchandise trade with Japan—that is, exports and imports—was more than $63 billion in 1982. Every American is affected by this trade. American consumers buy automobiles, televisions, cameras, film, pens, and watches. American companies buy copiers, machine tools, and robotics. The Japanese buy our agricultural products, lumber, coal, chemicals, computers, aircraft, petroleum and associated production equipment, sporting goods, and pharmaceuticals.

All of this trade—consumer and industrial goods sales, joint ventures, mergers, acquisitions, other investments, and government actions—requires that Americans and Japanese sit face to face and negotiate agreements. This has not been easy. Yet the explanations for our trade problems with Japan offered by Ambassador Mike Mansfield and others are at the macroeconomic or institutional level, that is, tariffs and quotas, government interference, labor, myopic business leadership, and the like. Certainly, these latter causes are important. But how much of the problem results from American ineptness at the international negotiation table?

More than twenty years ago anthropologist E. T. Hall warned: "When the American executive travels abroad to do business, he is frequently shocked to discover to what extent many variables of foreign behavior and custom complicate his efforts."[1] A few of our own business and government leaders have recently echoed this theme. For example, J. William Fulbright suggests that "our linguistic and cultural myopia is losing us friends, business, and respect in the world."[2] Still, we have only a superficial understanding of the difficulties involved in cross-cultural negotiations, and for good reason: problems at the negotiation table are difficult to observe and evaluate. Alternatively, government tax rates, increasing labor costs, and leadership attitudes are much more easily measured. Thus, we see an emphasis on institutional level solutions with little attention paid to the "typically ethnocentric American" sitting across the table from "inscrutable foreign customers" trying to negotiate an acceptable business contract. In this book Graham and Sano attempt to shed light on this circumstance. The topic is a worthy subject for investigation since Japanese-American business negotiations often fail for seemingly inexplicable reasons, and because most others have ignored such questions.

With the dramatic growth in international business activity during the last ten years, American executives have slowly adjusted their approaches to foreign markets. Early on, American executives were sent to live overseas and deal directly with foreign clients. The point of contact for the two cultures was often between an American representative and foreign client personnel. Thus, Americans were asked to live in a new environment and accomplish the difficult task of promoting communication and understanding not only between cultures but also between organizations. Generally, this strategy has been unsuccessful.

In response to these difficulties, American firms are increasingly hiring foreign nationals to represent their interests overseas. This moves the point of cross-cultural contact to within the firm where it can be more effectively managed. Consequently, the trend is for American executives (managers and technical experts) to take short trips to other countries.

Such a strategy for international trade neatly avoids the substantial problems of training executives to live in other cultures. We can now focus our attention on teaching executives how to negotiate with people from other countries. But there are still difficulties. First, knowledge and experience in one culture do not necessarily help in understanding other cultures. Different factors may be important in different places. Second, there are practical limitations on executive time. Often, management or technical people are required to participate in business negotiations in other countries on short notice. The focus of preparation is on commercial and technical issues, not on how to communicate effectively with foreigners.

In his research at USC, Graham has taken a unique approach to the study of cross-cultural business negotiations. He particularly has attempted to view Japanese-American business negotiations from several perspectives. During preliminary field work he interviewed experienced executives and observed business interactions in both the United States and Japan. Later, a negotiation experiment was conducted involving more than 200 American and Japanese businesspeople. Graham is presently extending his studies of international bargaining styles to include Taiwan, Brazil, and Mexico.

The real strength of this book lies in the synergy created by the integration of Graham's scholarly approach with Sano's breadth of experience in Japanese-American business negotiations and his personal understanding of Japan. Yoshi was born in Osaka and was educated in Japan prior to receiving degrees in economics and international business from USC and UCLA. In 1976 Yoshi joined the IBEAR program where, as associate director, he worked both in curriculum development and promotion of the IBEAR throughout the Pacific Basin.

Since 1980 Yoshi has worked for Ernst & Whinney and is now manager of Japanese Practice Development for the Western Region. Through such experiences Yoshi has a truly unique understanding of Japanese-American trade problems. He has seen first hand how American managers have been successful in dealings with Japanese clients and partners, and he has been witness to failures of executives on both sides of the Pacific.

Graham and Sano's book will go a long way toward helping American managers handle assignments in Japan. Managers, sales representatives, technical experts, and all business executives involved in commercial negotiations will benefit by reading this book. The knowledge presented here will aid Americans in establishing and maintaining economically and personally satisfying relationships with Japanese clients, partners, and suppliers.

Roy A. Herberger, Jr.
Dean, Edwin L. Cox School of Business
Southern Methodist University
Dallas, Texas

NOTES

1. E. T. Hall, "The Silent Language in Overseas Business," *Harvard Business Review* (May–June 1960): 87–96.
2. J. William Fulbright, "We're tongue-tied," *Newsweek*, July 30, 1979, p. 15.

ACKNOWLEDGMENTS

There are several people we must thank for their help in the creation of our book. Roy Herberger's influence and inspiration are evident throughout the text. Walter F. Beran and Donald B. Hadley at Ernst & Whinney provided the opportunity for Yoshi's experiences in international business negotiations. Moreover, both commented extensively on the original manuscript. Also providing insightful reviews of the manuscript were Peter A. Magowan and John H. Prinster of Safeway Stores, Inc.; Yasuhiro Hagihara and Hidetoshi Asakura of Graham and James, Attorneys; Yoshiaki Shibusawa of California First Bank; Setsuko Sugimachi of Mitsui Bank, Ltd.; and David A. Livdahl of Fenwick, Stone, Davis and West, Attorneys. The executives at Solar Turbines, Inc., subsidiary of Caterpillar Tractor Co., and particularly John Gerretsen, must be thanked for their cooperation and support. Much of Graham's research was funded by a grant to the USC School of Business from Toyota Motor Co. Mary C. Gilly at the University of California, Irvine, and Marilyn Sano helped in the editing process. Rene Gay at USC typed the original manuscript. David Barber at Ballinger helped in the production of the book. Carol Franco at Ballinger was our guide into the business of publishing and saw the value of our ideas from the onset.

Finally, we must thank our families—for they have lent us to this task. Thanks to all!

1 INTRODUCTION

THE AISATSU

The initial meeting was scheduled weeks in advance for a Thursday afternoon in the Japanese firm's corporate offices in Tokyo. The primary purpose was the introduction of a high-level American executive to the president of a Japanese firm in a typical Japanese *aisatsu* (a formal greeting). The principal American negotiator was a relatively young (early forties), recently promoted sales vice president of an American capital equipment manufacturer. The two firms were in the final stages of establishing an important agreement for distribution of the American products in Japan. Protocol dictated a visit by a high-level representative of the American firm. A visit by the vice president was convenient because at that time he was scheduled to tour some of his new areas of responsibility, including Japan.

I had spent the early part of the week with the American firm's Tokyo representative observing a variety of Japanese-American business meetings. Much of that activity involved preparations for the Thursday meeting, working with lower level executives of the Japanese firm to coordinate final details.

As Thursday approached things began to go wrong. Final approval of the distribution agreement from the U.S. corporate headquarters and legal counsel was expected before the meeting. However, the

1

Tokyo representative received news that, if the approval came at all, it would be delayed until after the vice president's arrival and scheduled meetings. This presented the ticklish problem of holding the scheduled meetings but avoiding making commitments—acting positive but not saying yes.

The American vice president was due to arrive in Tokyo Wednesday evening before the Thursday *aisatsu*. He was to be briefed regarding the commercial aspects of the deal by the company's Far East district sales manager accompanying him on the flight. The flight from Singapore was delayed twelve hours and the two executives arrived at their Tokyo hotel at 9:00 A.M. Thursday. The Tokyo representative and I met them for a quick breakfast at the hotel.

The Tokyo representative briefed his superiors on the recent developments. The three Americans decided on a strategy of "dancing" with the Japanese—avoiding discussion of business as long as possible and avoiding making any firm commitments.

This was the vice president's first visit to Japan. His previous international experiences were extensive and included business negotiations in Europe, the Middle East, and Africa. He appropriately asked the Tokyo representative about protocol and other cultural considerations. He was told generally not to worry and to just act naturally. He was also told that substantive business discussions were not appropriate at the *aisatsu*. Following the briefing the two senior executives retreated to their rooms to shower and take a rest before the 2:00 P.M. meeting.

The three representatives of the American firm and I arrived at the Japanese corporate offices at 2:00 P.M. We were greeted by a female employee in the uniform of the company. She escorted us to a nearby formal meeting room. The room was furnished in expensive but conservative easy chairs with several coffee tables. The sixteen chairs were arranged in a square. We were not asked to sit, and shortly after our arrival three Japanese executives entered the room. The executives whom I had met earlier in the week were assigned specific management responsibilities related to the distribution of the American products. Introductions were made and business cards exchanged, but in a relatively more formal manner than I had previously observed in other interactions with the same managers. The American vice president was treated with obvious respect. The seven of us chatted in English about travel from Singapore and other non-task-related matters.

Behavioral scientists tell us that Americans are relatively uncomfortable with obvious status distinctions. As the conversation progressed it became apparent that all four Americans (including myself) were unconsciously imitating the respectful and formal behaviors of the three Japanese, thus equalizing the initial status distinctions. About the time this interpersonal equalization had been completed, three more Japanese executives entered the room. These three were members of the president's executive staff, much older than the first three (late fifties) and treated with utmost respect by the first three Japanese. Because the Americans had successfully established an ambiance of status equality with the first three Japanese, there now existed a large status gap between the Americans and the three Japanese executive staff members. This again was an uncomfortable situation for the Americans, who began to try to establish status equality with the three new Japanese executives. However, before this status manipulation could be completed, the Japanese company president entered the room. The six Japanese already in the room acted most formally and respectfully, and thus, the status position of the Americans took another dip from which it never fully recovered.

Once again business cards were exchanged and formal introductions made. One of the first three Japanese acted as an interpreter for the Japanese president, even though the president spoke and understood English. The president asked us to be seated. We seated ourselves *in exact order of rank.* The interpreter sat on a stool between the two senior executives. The general attitude between the parties was friendly but polite. Tea and a Japanese orange drink were served.

The Japanese president controlled the interaction completely, asking questions of all the Americans through the interpreter. Attention of all participants was given to each speaker in turn. After this initial round of questions for all Americans, the Japanese president focused on developing a conversation with the American vice president. During this interaction an interesting pattern in nonverbal behaviors developed. The Japanese president would ask a question in Japanese. The interpreter then translated the question for the American vice president. While the interpreter spoke, the American's attention (gaze direction) was given to the interpreter. However, the Japanese president's gaze direction was at the American. Thus, the Japanese president could carefully and unobtrusively observe the American's facial expressions and nonverbal responses. Alternatively, when the American spoke the Japanese president had twice the response time. Because he understood English, he could formulate his responses during the translation process.

This interesting conversational interaction continued on non-task-related matters for several minutes, the Japanese viewing business discussions at an *aisatsu* as inappropriate and the Americans specifically avoiding business discussion for strategic reasons. The weight of the conversation was clearly directed toward the senior American executive by the Japanese president. The seating arrangement also served to focus everyone's attention on the American vice president, who often filled the gaps in the conversation. When the topic turned to golf, a favorite sport of the American, his mood noticeably improved. He mentioned the several golf courses in the local area of the American headquarters and an upcoming professional golf tournament.

Then, to everyone's disbelief, the American vice president invited the Japanese president to the Golf tournament when the president traveled to the United States *to sign the distribution agreement!* The American continued to talk about business and the distribution agreement and predicted a long and prosperous relationship between the two firms. The Japanese president courteously responded to the American's statements. He also ended the meeting shortly thereafter by excusing himself and suggesting moving to another conference room for a presentation by his executive staff.

It seemed incomprehensible that the American vice president would make such statements and commitments given his briefing prior to the *aisatsu.* A brief recap of the antecedent conditions helps to explain this major error. Four characteristics of the vice president seem to be relevant. He was younger than his Japanese counterpart by approximately twenty years. He was inexperienced in the Far East, particularly in Japan. He was physically fatigued after a long flight and little sleep. And finally he was unprepared, having been told to "act naturally" in his morning briefing. The process of the meeting also appears to have worked against the American. In particular, the hierarchical introductions and vertical status relations put him in an unfamiliar and uncomfortable status position. The Japanese president's use of the interpreter further disadvantaged him. Also, the vice president obviously felt the weight of both the conversational responsibility of answering questions and filling gaps and the distinct physical focus of attention.

Thus, contrary to the Americans' agreed game plan, a verbal commitment was made at the *aisatsu*. The district sales manager later explained to me the potential consequences of this faux pas. The most obvious was a loss of face by the Americans because business is never to be discussed at an *aisatsu*. Worse yet, if headquarters failed to agree with the vice president's commitments, the business with the Japanese firm would be finished. Even if headquarters did agree, the Tokyo sales representative lost an important degree of control over management of the relationship. Because the Tokyo sales representative and the vice president presented somewhat different positions to the Japanese group, the Japanese would tend to bypass the representative on important issues and contact the vice president directly. The district sales manager did mention one possible benefit of the error: the vice president would work harder to conclude the agreement once he returned to U.S. headquarters in the United States.

This description of an *aisatsu* is excerpted from John Graham's field notes taken during the initial stages of our six-year study of Japanese and American negotiation styles. Since then we have found that situations such as the one described occur all too frequently when Americans call on Japanese clients. We feel the major problem has to do with the "natural" behavior of American negotiators. This is a book primarily about an American style of business negotiation. The fact that such a style exists is not apparent until negotiation behaviors of Americans are compared to those of business executives in other countries. Thus, a second purpose of this book will be to compare the American negotiation style to that of perhaps our most important international trading partner, Japan.

As any American businessperson who has traveled to Japan will quickly point out, the Japanese have a style of bargaining distinctly their own. Discussion of these two very different styles of negotiations leads to the central theme of the book: American businesspeople, *by nature*, will have great difficulties bargaining with Japanese businessmen. When Americans travel to Japan to negotiate with prospective clients or partners, the natural bargaining behavior that achieves good results at home can cause major problems. Business negotiations in Japan will have to be handled differently and we intend the book to be a useful guide toward this end.

2 THE AMERICAN NEGOTIATION STYLE

Picture if you will the closing scenes of John Wayne's academy award winning performance in *True Grit.* Sheriff Rooster Cogburn sitting astride his chestnut mare, a Colt .45 in one hand, a Winchester .73 in the other, whiskey on his breath, reins in his teeth, stampeding across the Arkansas prairie straight into the sights and range of villains' guns. A face-to-face shootout with four bad guys, and sure enough, the John Wayne character comes through again.

Great entertainment, yes! We know it's all fantasy. We know that in real life Sheriff Rooster Cogburn would have ended up face down in the blood and dust, alongside his dead horse. But it's more fun to see the fantasy nonetheless.

Such scenes from movies, TV, and books influence our everyday behavior in subtle, but powerful ways. We tend to model our behavior after such John Wayne figures. And when everyone else plays the same game, the bluff and bravado often work. But such behavior becomes a problem when we sit face to face across a negotiation table with business executives who haven't grown up on a steady diet of John Wayne Saturday matinees. Our minds play out the familiar scenes. But instead of six-guns and Bowie knives, our weapons are words, questions, threats and promises, laughter, and confrontation. We anticipate victory, despite the odds—four against one is no problem. But we are often disappointed to find it's not the movies. It's a real life business negotiation. At stake are the profits of our companies, not to mention our own compensation and reputation. And like a real-life sheriff, we could lose.

This scenario repeats itself with increasing frequency as American enterprise turns more global. The John Wayne bargaining style, which has served us well in conference rooms across the country, does us great disservice in conference rooms across the sea.

THE JOHN WAYNE STYLE

Probably no single statement better summarizes the American negotiation style than "shoot first, ask questions later," a phrase straight out of a Saturday afternoon Western. But the roots of the American negotiation style run much deeper than movies and television reruns. To understand the American approach to bargaining, we must consider more basic aspects of our cultural background—in particular, our immigrant heritage, our frontier history, and finally, much of the training in our present-day business and law schools.

Throughout its history, America has been a nation influenced by its immigrants. Certainly the continuous mixing of ideas and perspectives brought from across the seas has enriched all our experiences. Every newcomer has had to work hard to succeed; thus the powerful work ethic of America. Another quality of our immigrant forefathers was a fierce independence—a characteristic necessary for survival in the wide open spaces. But this latter quality does us disservice at the negotiation table. Negotiation is by definition a situation of interdependence—a situation that Americans have never handled well.

We inherit much of this mentality from our frontier history. "Move out West where there's elbow room," runs the conventional wisdom of the first 150 years of our nation's existence. Americans as a group haven't had much practice negotiating because they have always been able to go elsewhere if conflicts arose.

The long distances between people allowed a social system to develop with not only fewer negotiations but also shorter ones. A day-long horseback ride to the general store or stockyard didn't favor long, drawn out negotiations. It was important to settle things quickly and leave no loose ends to the bargain. "Tell me yes, or tell me no—but give me a straight answer." Candor, laying your cards on the table, was highly valued and expected in the Old West. And it still is today in our boardrooms and classrooms.

What goes on in the classrooms in our business and law schools has a strong influence on our negotiation style. Throughout the American educational system we are taught to compete, both academically and on the sporting field. Adversary relationships and winning are essential themes of the American socialization process. But nowhere in the American educational system is competition and winning more important than in case discussions in our law and business classrooms. They who make the best arguments, marshal the best evidence, or demolish the opponents' arguments win both the respect of classmates and high marks. Such skills will be important at the negotiation table, but the most important negotiation skills aren't taught or are at best shamefully underemphasized in both business and legal training. We don't teach our students how to ask questions, how to get information, how to listen, or how to use questioning as a powerful persuasive strategy. In fact, few of us realize that in most places in the world, the one who asks the questions controls the process of negotiation and thereby accomplishes more in bargaining situations.

A combination of attitudes, expectations, and habitual behaviors constitutes the John Wayne negotiation style. Each characteristic is discussed separately below, but it should be understood that each factor is connected to the others to form the complex foundation for a series of negotiation strategies and tactics typically American. We hope it is obvious that what we are talking about is the typical or dominant behavior of American negotiators. Obviously not every American executive is impatient, a poor listener, or argumentative. Nor does every American manager encounter difficulties during international negotiations. But many do, particularly when compared with businesspeople from other countries.

I Can Go It Alone

Most American executives feel they should be able to handle any negotiation situation by themselves. "Four Japanese versus one American is no problem. I don't need any help. I can think and talk fast enough to get what I want, what the company needs." So goes the John Wayne rationalization. And there's an economic justification: "Why take more people than I need?" Another more subtle reason might be: "Why not take full credit for success?" Often, then, the American side is outnumbered when it shows up for business discussions.

Being outnumbered or, worse yet, being alone is a severe disadvantage in a negotiation situation. Several things are going on at once — talking, listening, preparing arguments and explanations, formulating questions, and seeking approval. Numbers help in obvious ways with most of the above. Indeed, on a Japanese negotiation team one member is often assigned the task of carefully listening with no speaking responsibilities at all. Consider for a moment how carefully you might listen to a speaker if you didn't have to think up a response to his or her next question. But perhaps the most important reason for having greater, or at least equal, numbers on your side is the powerful, subtle influence of nodding heads and positive facial expressions. Negotiation is very much a social activity, and the approval and agreement of others (friend and foe) can have critical effects on negotiation outcomes. Numbers can also be a subtle indicator of the seriousness and commitment of both parties to a negotiation.

Just Call Me John

Americans more than any other cultural group value informality and equality in human relations. The emphasis on first names is only the tip of the iceberg. We go out of our way to make our clients feel comfortable by playing down status distinctions such as titles and by eliminating unnecessary formalities such as lengthy introductions. But all too often we succeed in making only ourselves feel comfortable while our clients become uneasy or even annoyed.

In Japanese society, interpersonal relationships are vertical; that is, in almost all two-person relationships a difference in status exists. The basis for this status distinction may be any of several factors: age, sex, place of education, position in a firm, which firm, or even industry of employment. For example, the president of the number one firm in an industry holds a higher status position than the president of the number two firm in the same industry. The Japanese are very much aware of such distinctions and of their positions in the hierarchy. And for good reason, knowledge of their status positions dictates how they will act during interpersonal interactions. Thus, it is easy to understand the importance of exchanging business cards in Japan; such a ritual clearly establishes the status relationships and lets each person know which role to play. The roles of the higher status position and lower status position are very different, even to the extent that different words are used to express the same idea depending on which person makes the statement. For example, a buyer would say *otaku* (your company), while a seller would say *on sha* (your great company). Status relations dictate not only what can be said, but how it is said.

Such rules for conducting business discussions are difficult for Americans to understand. We can perhaps get by with our informal, egalitarian style when we're dealing with foreigners in the United States. However, we only make things difficult for ourselves and our companies by asking executives in Tokyo, Paris, or London to "just call me John (or Mary)."

Pardon My French

Americans aren't adept at speaking foreign languages. Often we aren't even apologetic about it. We rightly argue that English is the international language, particularly with regard to technology and science. Wherever we go we expect to find someone who speaks English. Often we do; but when we don't, we are left to the mercy of third-party translators.

Even when our clients, partners, or suppliers do speak English we are at a disadvantage at the negotiation table. First, the use of interpreters gives the other side some subtle but very real advantages. For example, foreign executives will sometimes use interpreters even when they have a good understanding of English. This permits them to observe our nonverbal responses. Alternatively, when we speak, the executives have longer to respond. Because they understand English, they can formulate their responses during the translation process.

Having to bargain in English puts a second, very powerful negotiation tool in the hands of our opponents. On the face of it, bargaining in our first language should be an advantage, but even the most powerful argument fizzles when the other side responds, "Sorry,

I'm not sure I understand. Can you repeat that please?" Bargainers listening in a second language have more freedom to use the tactic of selective understanding. It also works when they speak. Previous commitments are more easily dissolved with the excuse, "that isn't exactly what I meant."

A third disadvantage concerns our assumptions about those who speak English well. When facing a group of foreign executives it is natural to assume that the one who speaks English best is also the most intelligent and influential in the group. This is seldom the case in foreign business negotiations. Yet, we often direct our persuasive appeals and attention toward the one who speaks the best English, thus accomplishing little.

Check With The Home Office

It is not always easy to identify the key decisionmaker in international business negotiations. Indeed, American bargainers become very upset when halfway through a negotiation the other side says, "I'll have to check with the home office," thus making it known that the decisionmakers aren't even at the negotiation table. In such a situation, Americans feel they've wasted time or even been misled.

Having limited authority at the negotiation table is a common circumstance overseas and can be a useful bargaining tactic. In reality the foreign executive is saying, "In order to get me to compromise you have to convince not only me but also my boss, who is 5,000 miles away." Thus, your arguments must be most persuasive. Additionally, such a bargaining tactic helps to maintain harmony at the negotiation table by letting the home office take the blame for saying no.

But such tactics go against the grain of the American bargaining style. Americans pride themselves in having full authority to make a deal. After all, John Wayne never had to check with the home office!

Get To The Point

As mentioned earlier, Americans don't like to beat around the bush but prefer to get to the heart of the matter as quickly as possible. Unfortunately, what is considered the heart of the matter in a business negotiation varies across cultures. In every country we have found business negotiations to proceed in the following four stages:

1. nontask sounding;
2. task-related exchange of information;
3. persuasion; and
4. concessions and agreement.

The first stage includes all those activities that help establish a rapport. It does *not* include information related to the business of the meeting. The information exchanged in the second stage of business negotiations regards the parties' needs and preferences. The third stage involves their attempts to change each other's mind through the use of various persuasive tactics. The final stage is the consummation of an agreement which is often the summation of a series of concessions or smaller agreements.

From the American point of view, the heart of the matter is the third stage—persuasion. We have a tendency to go through the first two stages quickly. We do talk about golf or the weather or family, but relative to other cultures, we spend little time doing so. We state our needs and preferences and we're quick about that too. We tend to be more interested in logical arguments than in the people with whom we're negotiating.

In many other countries the heart of the matter is not so much information and persuasion as the people involved. In Japan, much time is spent getting to know one another. Since the Japanese would prefer not to depend on a legal system to iron out conflicts, a strong relationship of trust must be established before business can begin. Americans new to the Japanese way are particularly susceptible to what we call the "wristwatch syndrome." In the United States, looking at your watch usually gets things moving along. In Japan, impatience signals apprehension and thus necessitates even longer periods of nontask sounding.

Lay Your Cards On The Table

Americans expect honest information at the negotiation table. When we don't get it, negotiations often end abruptly. We also understand that, like dollars, information must be traded. "You tell me what you want and I'll tell you what we want." The problem with this is that negotiators in other countries may have different attitudes and values about "honest information." In Japan it can be very difficult to get a straight answer for two reasons. First, the Japanese team may not have decided what it wants out of the deal. Second, if the answer is no, the Japanese side may not be willing to say so. Because it is the Japanese style to avoid conflict and embarrassment they may sidestep, beat around the bush, or even remain silent. We misread and often feel misled by such subtle negative responses. Japanese executives, particularly those educated since World War II with international experience, say they are learning to value directness. But here too the tradition is a long one and is a powerful influence on behavior at the negotiation table.

Don't Just Sit There, Speak Up

Americans are uncomfortable with silence during negotiations. This may seem a minor point, but we have often witnessed Americans getting themselves into trouble—particularly in Japan—by filling silent periods.

The American style of conversation consists of few long silent periods—that is, ten seconds or greater. Alternatively, the Japanese style includes occasional long periods of silence, particularly in response to an impasse. We have found that American negotiators react to Japanese silence in one of two ways. Either they make some kind of a concession or they fill the gap in the conversation with a persuasive appeal. The latter tactic has two counterproductive results: (1) the American does most of the talking, and (2) he or she learns little about the Japanese point of view.

Don't Take No For An Answer

Persistence is highly valued by Americans. We are taught from the earliest age to never give up. In sports, classroom, or boardroom, we are taught to be aggressive and to win. Subsequently, we view a negotiation as something to be won. We expect a negotiation to have a definite conclusion, a signed contract. Moreover, we are dissatisfied and distressed if we don't get the bigger piece of pie. But even worse than losing a negotiation is not concluding a negotiation. We can take a loss—consoling ourselves that we'll do better next time—but not the ambiguity of no outcome.

This competitive, adversarial, "persistence pays" view of negotiation is not necessarily shared by our foreign clients and vendors. Negotiations are viewed in many countries as a means of establishing long-term commercial relations that have no definite conclusions. Negotiations are considered a cooperative effort where interdependence is manifest and each side tries to add to the pie.

One Thing At a Time

Americans tend to attack a complex negotiation task sequentially. That is, they separate the issues and settle them one at a time. For example, we have heard American bargainers say, "let's settle the quantity first and then discuss price." Thus, in an American negotiation, the final agreement is a sum of the several concessions made on individual issues, and progress can be measured easily. "We're halfway done when we're through half the issues." However, in other countries, particularly Far Eastern cultures, concessions tend to be made only at the end of a negotiation. All issues are discussed using a holistic approach, and nothing is settled until the end.

Because negotiators on the other side "never seem to commit themselves to anything," American executives invariably feel that little progress is being made during cross-cultural negotiations. Agreements are often unexpected and often follow unnecessary concessions by American bargainers.

A Deal Is a Deal

When an American makes an agreement, he or she is expected to honor the agreement no matter what the circumstances. But agreements are viewed differently in other parts of the world. W. H. Newman aptly sums up the problem:

> In some parts of the world it is impolite to openly refuse to do something that has been requested by another person. What a Westerner takes as a commitment may be little more than friendly conversation. In some societies, it is understood that today's commitment may be superseded by a conflicting request received tomorrow, especially if that request comes from a highly

influential person. In still other situations, agreements merely signify intention and have little relation to capacity to perform; as long as the person tries
to perform he feels no pangs of conscience, and he makes no special effort, if
he is unable to fulfill the agreement. Obviously, such circumstances make
business dealings much more uncertain, especially for new undertakings.[1]

I Am What I am

Most Americans take pride in determination, not changing one's
mind even given difficult circumstances. John Wayne's character and
behavior was constant and predictable. He treated everyone and
every situation with an action-oriented, forthright style. John Wayne
could never be accused of being a chameleon—changing colors with
changing environments.

Many American bargainers take the same attitudes with them to
the negotiation table. Competition, persistence, and determination
no matter what. But during international business negotiations, in-
flexibility can be a fatal flaw. There simply isn't a strategy or tactic
that always works. Different countries and different personalities
require different approaches.

Most Americans are not aware of a native negotiation style. We
tend to perceive bargaining behavior in terms of personality: the
Texas "good ole boy" approach or the Wall Street "city slicker"
approach or the California "laid back" style. But when viewed
through the eyes of our foreign clients and partners, we Americans
have an approach to bargaining all our own. And this distinct flavor
we bring to the bargaining table, this John Wayne style, is the source
of many problems overseas. We must learn to adjust our behavior and
gain an appreciation for subtler forms of negotiation.

NOTE TO CHAPTER 2

1. W. H. Newman, "Cultural Assumptions Underlying U.S. Management Con-
cepts," in *Management in International Context*, J. L. Massie, J. Luytjons,
and N. W. Hazen, eds. (New York: Harper & Row, 1972), p. 75.

3 THE JAPANESE NEGOTIATION STYLE

The Japanese negotiation style is perhaps the most distinctive in the world. Moreover, contrary to what one might expect, the Japanese style is also far different from negotiation styles in China and Korea, Japan's closest neighbors. Compared to the aggressive haggling typical of Korean and Chinese businesspeople, the subtle, low-key bargaining of Japanese executives appears foreign indeed.

The historical and cultural roots of the Japanese negotiation style run far deeper than those of the American style. Their history is much longer and relatively uninfluenced from the outside. Another characteristic that sets the Japanese style apart from all others is the suitability of the Japanese style for international use. An important aspect of the Japanese style of business negotiations includes adapting bargaining behaviors to those of the host country or firm. This idea will be developed later in the book. For now, let's consider the historical and cultural foundations of the Japanese negotiation style.

THE ROOTS OF THE JAPANESE STYLE OF BUSINESS NEGOTIATION

The natural environment of Japan has had a pervasive influence on the character of social systems, personal relationships and, yes, even the process of business negotiations. Three environmental factors are

17

salient: (1) the insular and mountainous geography, (2) the dense population, and (3) the importance of rice as the basic food crop.

Throughout its history Japan has been an isolated country. Until the fifteenth century the surrounding seas formed a substantial barrier preventing invasions and limiting influence from the Asian continent. Even with the dramatic changes throughout the rest of the world brought about by Western European maritime power in the sixteenth century, the political policies of the Tokugawa Shogunate kept foreigners out of the country. Indeed, Japan was the country least influenced by Western European culture through the mid-nineteenth century. And not only did the maritime barriers keep foreigners out, but they also kept Japanese from leaving. Thus social systems and personal relationships developed in a concentrated environment where geography dictated that cooperation was essential. Ethnicity, cultural values, and behavioral norms are therefore uniquely consistent and homogeneous.

The mountains in Japan have always made travel within the country difficult, adding further to the isolation of social groups. Because of the mountains, only about 10 percent of the land can be cultivated. Japan is the most densely populated of all countries in the world with respect to people per square mile of arable land. This crowding has fostered a tightly organized society that highly values obedience and cooperation. Crowding does not permit the aggressive independence and equality so characteristic in the United States.

The final environmental factor influencing values and behaviors in Japan is the historical importance of rice cultivation. Until 100 years ago, five-sixths of the population of Japan was employed in rice cultivation. Rice production requires community effort and cooperation. Irrigation, planting, and harvesting are most efficiently accomplished with the participation of groups of families. Thus, the small group has evolved as the salient social unit in Japan. Individual needs and desires are deemphasized in favor of one's social unit. In the historical agrarian society the family and village were key. Now in Japan, one's family and one's work group are central. Loyalty and consensus decisionmaking are key elements that bind such groups together.

Because of this unique combination of environmental influences, a social system has evolved in Japan that avoids conflict and promotes harmony. And as in America, classroom behavior is influenced by and tends to reinforce these cultural values and behavioral norms.

Lively case discussions are not part of the educational experience in Japan. Rather, professors present lectures with no questions and feedback from students. Listening skills and obedience, rather than debating skills and independent thinking, are rewarded in the Japanese educational system. It should be understood that the Japanese negotiation style characterized in the paragraphs to follow is deeply influenced by and reflects these salient environmental factors and the values and social structures associated with them.

TATE SHAKAI (Living and Working in a Vertical Society)

Perhaps the most important difference between the Japanese negotiation style and others, particularly the American, concerns status relationships. At the interpersonal level the bases for the status distinction might be age, sex, education, or occupation. The power position in business relationships has more to do with size and prestige of the company, industry structure (e.g., number of competitors), and, very often, which company is the buyer. There are cases when sellers are more powerful—large manufacturers versus small retailers—but most often Japanese buyers expect and receive deference from Japanese sellers. Indeed, in Japan the buyer is said to be "kinger." Note the following excerpt from a pamphlet provided by the Manufactured Imports Promotion Organization of Japan:

> In Japan, as in other countries, the "buyer is king," only here he or she is "kinger." Here, the seller, beyond meeting pricing, delivery, special specifications, and other usual conditions, must do as much as possible to meet a buyer's wishes. . . . Many companies doing business in Japan make it a practice to deliver more than called for under the terms of their contracts.[1]

The key point here is that the roles of the buyer and seller are very different in Japan. Status relations dictate what is said and what bargaining strategies may be used during Japanese business negotiations. The norms of behavior for the seller are much different than for the buyer.

In America the way in which status distinctions affect how we behave is almost the opposite of that in Japan. In Japan people at all levels feel uncomfortable if status distinctions do not exist or are not understood. But in our egalitarian American society, we often go out of our way to establish an interpersonal equality. There is little distinction between roles and relatively few rules for adjusting behavior.

Americans expect to, and do, affect business outcomes at the negotiation table. For Japanese, negotiation is more of a ritual, with actions predetermined and prespecified by status relations.

AMAE (Indulgent Dependency)

Hierarchical personal and business relationships are difficult for Americans to understand. "Doesn't the lower status seller get taken advantage of? That's what would happen in the United States." However, understanding an additional aspect of Japanese hierarchical relationships is essential for full appreciation of the Japanese business system. It is true that Japanese buyers have the freedom to choose the deal they want. They will get little argument from the Japanese sellers. But along with this freedom goes an implicit responsibility to consider the needs of the sellers. Japanese sellers can trust the buyers not to take advantage of them. This theme of *amae* is woven into every aspect of Japanese society. Consider, for example, the relationship between management and labor. Management has much more control over labor in Japan than in the United States. But with that control comes a large measure of responsibility for the welfare of the labor force, exceeding that in America.

In Japan buyers take care of sellers. Buyers consider the needs of sellers before making demands that sellers defer to. In America, conversely, we all take care of ourselves. If buyers make unreasonable demands, they will most likely hear an argument.

NAGAI TSUKIAI (Long-Term Relationships)

Another aspect of business relationships in Japan that influences negotiation behavior regards the importance and expectation of long-term relationships. The fact that Japanese managers are more predisposed than American managers to take a long view of business affairs has been given much attention. The importance of establishing long-term relations is grounded in the cultural heritage of being isolated and having no other place to go. Personal and group relationships are for life and therefore entered into slowly, carefully, and in a socially prescribed way. The same is true for business relationships.

This aspect of Japanese values has two important implications for business negotiations with Japanese clients or partners. First, the Japanese side will want to spend more time getting to know prospective American associates. They will be more willing to invest time and money in negotiation preliminaries and rituals. The second and perhaps the more important implication regards the structure and presentation of the business deal itself. Japanese bargainers will be looking for long-term commitments. Short-run profits are important, but secondary to a long-run business association benefiting both sides.

SHINYO (Gut Feeling)

In the previous chapter we mentioned four stages of the negotiation process: nontask sounding, task-related information exchange, persuasion, and concessions and agreement. We also pointed out that, from the American point of view, the persuasion stage is the heart of the matter. It is different in Japan. Compared to Americans, Japanese spend a considerable amount of time in nontask sounding activities. The Japanese view the time and money spent in the initial stages of bargaining as an important investment.

The typical Japanese negotiation involves a series of nontask interactions and even ceremonial gift giving. The *aisatsu* described in Chapter 1 is prescribed behavior in Japan. Moreover, witness the recent attention given to the very large *kosai-hi* (literally, entertainment expenses) typical of business dealings in Japan. "While the Japanese defense budget is 0.9 percent of the country's GNP, corporate wining and dining accounts for 1.5 percent of the total national output."[2] To the American critic this may seem extravagant. However, the Japanese place great importance on establishing a harmonious relationship. This helps them avoid expensive litigation if things go wrong, which seems more and more common in the United States.

NANIWABUSHI (A Seller's Approach)

In Japan, information exchange during the second stage of negotiations is generally unidirectional. Sellers describe in great detail what they need, and buyers consider this information and make a decision. Sellers don't object or question the decision because they can trust the buyers to take care of them. Thus, the information flows principally from sellers to buyers.

Robert March, at Aoyama Gakin University in Tokyo, explains that the seller's agenda is often ordered like a Japanese narrative chant going back to the fifteenth century; a *naniwabushi* (both the chant and the negotiation approach) consists of three phases. "The opening, which is called *kikkake*, gives the general background of the story and tells what the people involved are thinking or feeling. Following this is the *seme*, an account of critical events. Finally, there is the *urei*, which expresses pathos and sorrow at what has happened or what is being requested."[3] The request comes last, after long explanation of the reasons why it is being made.

Alternatively, the American style of information exchange we have observed starts with the request (without the sorrow), and the explanation is provided only if necessary. American persuasive appeals are couched in terms of "you should . . ." rather than the Japanese "my company needs. . . ." To the American mind the *naniwabushi* seems melodramatic and a waste of time. However, this is the kind of behavior higher status buyers expect from lower status sellers. It is the kind of behavior that makes Japanese negotiators feel comfortable.

We have seen many examples of this approach to business negotiation. One case stands out. Safeway Stores, Inc., and Allied Import Company (AIC is a consortium of four of Japan's major retailers: JUSCO, UNY, Izumiya, and Chujitsuya) were discussing an agreement for the distribution of Safeway products in Japan. The Japanese presentation followed the *naniwabushi* approach. All aspects of the partnership had been agreed upon except for the exclusivity provisions. That is, the AIC representatives wanted to be the sole distributor of Safeway products in Japan. The presidents of the four Japanese companies had flown into San Francisco International Airport in preparation for signing ceremonies scheduled for that day. Yet, still no agreement had been reached regarding the exclusivity provision. Finally, at the last minute the head Japanese negotiator resorted to *urei*, and "cried on the shoulder" of an executive vice-president of Safeway, using an emotion drenched personal appeal. Thus, the time pressure and the *urei* broke the impasse; the deal was consummated that day with the Japanese receiving the exclusive rights of distribution.

BANANA NO TATAKI URI
(The Banana Sale Approach)

In the days of street vendors in Japan banana salesmen were notorious for asking outrageous prices and quickly lowering the prices when faced with buyers' objections. The term *banana no tataki uri* is now used in Japan to describe a similar approach taken by Japanese businesspeople. But instead of bananas, factories, distribution chains, even banks are sometimes bargained for using the "banana sale" approach. Japanese executives are more likely to use such a tactic during international negotiations because they don't know what to expect from foreign buyers and they feel that it's safer to leave room to maneuver.

WA (Maintaining Harmony)

Western negotiators universally complain about the difficulties of getting feedback from Japanese negotiators. There are three explanations for this complaint. First, the Japanese value interpersonal harmony or *wa* over frankness. Second, the Japanese perhaps have not come to a consensus regarding the offer or counteroffer. Third, Westerners tend to miss the subtle but clear signals given by the Japanese.

Wa, like *amae*, is one of the central values of the Japanese culture. Negative responses to negotiation proposals are principally nonexistent, and when they are given, they are given very subtly. We've all heard the classic story about the Japanese response of "we'll think it over" to an American's request. A simple response like this usually means no in American terms, for if the Japanese really wanted to think it over he would explain the details of the decisionmaking process and the reason for the delay. A Japanese negotiator would be, however, loathe to use the word "no." Indeed, one Japanese scholar, Keiko Ueda, has described sixteen ways to avoid saying no in Japan (see Table 3–1).

Regarding the ambiguous responses (see items 13 and 14 in Table 3–1), Japanese negotiators follow the cultural double standard of *tatemae* and *honne*. *Tatemae* can be translated as "truthful" (or official stance) and *honne* as "true mind" (or real intentions). It is im-

Table 3-1. Sixteen Ways the Japanese Avoid Saying No.

1. Vague "no"
2. Vague and ambiguous "yes" or "no"
3. Silence
4. Counter question
5. Tangential responses
6. Exiting (leaving)
7. Lying (equivocation or making an excuse—sickness, previous obligation, etc.)
8. Criticizing the question itself
9. Refusing the question
10. Conditional "no"
11. "Yes, but . . . "
12. Delaying answers (e.g., "We will write you a letter.")
13. Internally "yes," externally "no"
14. Internally "no," externally "yes"
15. Apology
16. The equivalent of the English "no"—primarily used in filling out forms, *not* in conversation

Source: Keiko Ueda, "Sixteen Ways to Avoid Saying "No" in Japan," in J.C. Condon and M. Saito, eds., *Intercultural Encounters in Japan* (Tokyo: Simul Press, 1974), pp. 185–192.

portant for Japanese to be polite and to communicate the *tatemae* while reserving the possibly offending, but also informative, *honne.* Additionally, this difference in the Japanese value system manifests itself in statements by Japanese negotiators in retrospective interviews. The Japanese often describe Americans as honest and frank, but to the point of discomfort for the Japanese. Finally, eye contact is much less frequent during Japanese negotiations, limiting leakage of potentially offending feelings and keeping intact the *honne.* To the American point of view this distinction between *tatemae* and *honne* seems hypocritical. However, the discrepancy is borne by the Japanese in good conscience and in the interest of the all-important *wa.*

RINGI KESSAI (Decisionmaking by Consensus)

Because of the importance of *wa* it is very difficult to get a "no" from a Japanese client. But because of group decisionmaking by consensus, it may also be difficult to get a "yes." Often, the Japanese side simply hasn't made up its mind.

In the voluminous comparative management literature, much has been made of the bottom-up approach to decisionmaking typical in Japanese organizations. It has the disadvantage of slowing down the decisionmaking, but the advantage of quick and orchestrated implementation. Moreover, this approach to decisionmaking has proved very successful in coordinating group efforts in modern companies as well as the traditional rice-growing agricultural communities. However, it has also been a substantial stumbling block and source of frustration for executives of American companies dealing with Japanese firms.

In business schools in the United States we teach the importance of identifying the key decisionmakers in an organization. In marketing terms, we look for the key buying influences. Generally, these key executives are located higher up in the organization. Once the key decisionmakers have been identified, special persuasive efforts are directed toward them. We try to determine the special interests (commercial and personal) of these key individuals, and communications are tailored accordingly.

Such an approach isn't likely to work in Japan. The decisionmaking power isn't centralized in key or high positions. Rather, the decisionmaking power is spread throughout the organization, and all executives involved in or influenced by the deal are important. All of them will have to be convinced that your proposal is the best before anything happens. The key buying influence in Japan is the executive who says no. Thus, the typical business negotiation in Japan will include talking to more people and will require repetition of the same information and persuasive appeals—much to the frustration of impatient Americans.

For American bargainers perhaps the greatest source of frustration associated with the consensus style of decisionmaking has to do with the difficulty of getting feedback. American bargainers asking, "What do you think of our proposal, or our counteroffer" often receive no answer. The Japanese are not being cagey, or coy, or dishonest; more often than not, a consensus has not been reached and Japanese negotiators (even senior people) are simply unwilling and unable to speak for the group.

ISHIN–DENSHIN (Communication Without Words)

The third reason foreigners complain about little feedback from Japanese negotiators has to do with the importance of nonverbal communication and subtlety in Japanese history, society, and business talk. Japan's ethnic homogeneity, isolation, and tradition of lifetime personal relationships with daily contact all permit the use of very subtle forms of communications. Subtlety is not only possible in such a fixed social system but is also required from the standpoint of *wa*.

America's tradition as a melting pot and the general transience of our personal relations make explicit communication necessary. Words are considered to be the most important vehicle of communication. In Japan much more is communicated nonverbally—through tone of voice, eye contact, silence, body movements, and the like. It's difficult for Americans to appreciate this difference in communication style and the importance of nonverbal channels in Japan. Takeo Doi, at the University of Tokyo, explains that in Japan the most important information, the content of the communication, is transmitted via nonverbal channels.[4] The verbal communication provides a context for the central information. The opposite is true in the United States, where communications researchers think of nonverbal signals as providing a context for the words spoken, the content of communication.

From the American point of view this Japanese mode of communication is incomprehensible. We know that nonverbal communication is very important, but how can a delivery date or a purchase price be communicated nonverbally? The explanation goes back to the concept of *shinyo* (gut feeling). To the Japanese, the key information in a negotiation concerns the qualities of the long-term, personal relationships that exist in the context of the business deal. The long discussion of minute details so prevalent in Japanese negotiations provides a context for development of comfortable personal relationships and a positive *shinyo*. And this *shinyo* is what makes the business deal go or not. Information about *shinyo* is communicated nonverbally and subtly. Delivery dates and purchase prices, which must be communicated verbally, are important; but these details are not the critical information in a Japanese business deal. So, Americans bargaining with Japanese are not only looking for the less important information but are also focusing on the wrong channel of communication. Thus, we have another explanation for the difficulty Americans have in getting feedback from Japanese clients and partners.

Kazuma Uyeno further explains the importance of nonverbal communication in his definition of *hara-gei:*

> Anatomically, *hara* is the abdomen or stomach. Used in figures of speech, the word can mean the heart or the mind of a man but not of a woman. *Hara* appears in a large number of expressions.
>
> The author who devoted a whole book to *hara-gei* (stomach art) would probably say that it is presumptuous to try to explain in just a few lines this Japanese problem-solving technique. *Hara-gei* may be explained as a technique for solving a problem through negotiation between two individuals without the use of direct words. You don't reveal to the other party what is in your *hara* but you unmistakably and effectively communicate your purpose, desire, demand, intention, advice or whatever through *hara-gei*.
>
> To do this, you bring into play psychology, intuition and your knowledge of the other party's personality, background, ambitions, personal connections, etc. and also what the other party knows about you. Only people with plenty of experience and cool nerves can make it succeed, but a lot of communication between Japanese in high positions is through *hara-gei*.[5]

NEMAWASHI (Preparing the Roots)

"Care to prepare the roots and the tree grows tall and strong," is an old Japanese saying. Its traditional wisdom holds critical importance for Americans bargaining with Japanese executives. The idea is that in Japan what goes on at the negotiation table is really a ritual approval of what has already been decided before, through numerous individual conversations in restaurants, bath houses, and offices. In Japan the negotiation table is not a place for changing minds. Persuasive appeals are not appropriate or effectual. If an impasse is reached, typical Japanese responses are silence, a change of subject, a request to consult the home office, or any of the several options for avoiding saying no. All members of the group must be consulted before new concessions or commitments are made.

As mentioned in the last chapter, the John Wayne approach to business negotiations is almost the opposite. Americans *do* expect minds to change at the negotiation table. Why else have the meeting?

When an impasse arises we use our best arguments and persuasive appeals to change the other side's point of view. Although the *nema-washi* approach is often used in the United States—we sometimes call it lobbying—and it may often be the smart strategy, it is not the norm.

SHOKAI-SHA (Introducer), CHUKAI-SHA (Mediator)

In his book, *The Japanese Way of Doing Business*, Boye DeMente mentions the importance of friendly and neutral third parties in establishing relationships and settling disputes between Japanese firms.[6] This is not a new idea in the West, but in Japan the functions of *shokai-sha* and *chukai-sha* are institutionalized.

Generally, business relationships in Japan are established only through the proper connections and associated introductions. "Cold calls" are simply not made. Instead, a third party (often a bank or trading company executive) familiar with both parties arranges and attends the initial meeting. This third party is called *shokai-sha* in Japan. At later stages in the negotiation, if things go wrong, another outside party or *chukai-sha* may be asked to mediate the conflicts. The *shokai-sha* will usually act in both capacities. Only in rare instances will the *shokai-sha* feel it necessary to call in another person to act as *chukai-sha*.

In the recent General Motors-Toyota joint venture, an executive vice-president of a major Japanese trading company called on executives in GM's Product Planning Department prior to the negotiations. He had worked previously with GM executives and was partially responsible for the American company's recent investment in Isuzu Motors. His trading company had worked with Toyota frequently in the past. He also participated in the initial discussion between the two firms. Because of his connections with both companies, this particular executive was the ideal *shokai-sha*.

THE SPECIAL PROBLEM FOR AMERICAN SELLERS

A special point of conflict exists when American sellers call on Japanese buyers. Given the horizontal relationship between American negotiators and the vertical relationship between Japanese negotiators, what happens in cross-cultural negotiations? It is our belief that a Japanese seller and an American buyer will get along fine, while the American seller and Japanese buyer will have great problems. Moreover, we believe this consideration to be a key factor in our trade difficulties with Japan. Our observations in the field and in the management laboratory (summarized in Table 3-2) provide strong evidence for such a proposition.

Table 3-2. Key Points of Conflict between American and Japanese Business Negotiation Styles.

Category	American	Japanese
Basic Cultural Values	competition	cooperation
	individual decision-making and action	group decisionmaking and action
	horizontal business relations	vertical business relations
	independence	*amae*
Negotiation Processes		
1. Nontask sounding	short	long, expensive
	informal	formal
2. Task-related exchange of information	"fair" first offers	"banana sale" first offers include room to maneuver
	full authority	limited authority
	"cards on the table"	*tatemae* and *honne*
	explicit communication	implicit communication
3. Persuasion	aggressive, persuasive tactics (threats, promises, arguments, and logic)	*nemawashi* and *chukai-sha*
	"you need this"	*naniwabushi*
4. Concessions and agreements	sequential	holistic
	goal = "good deal"	goal = long-term relationship

When Japanese sellers come to America to market their products, they naturally assume the lower status position, act accordingly (showing great deference for the American buyer), and a sale is made. Initially, Japanese sellers are taken advantage of. After all, they expect American buyers to respect their needs. But in any case, a relationship is established between firms. The door is open and the Japanese sellers have the opportunity to learn the American way, to adjust their behavior, and to establish a more viable long-term relationship.

Such a conception of the Japanese experience in America is supported by both field interviews and experiences and by our laboratory observations. Universally, Japanese executives in the United States report that their companies "took a beating" when entering the American market. But they also report adjusting their business and negotiation practices to fit the American system. Moreover, in the management laboratory the Japanese were more likely to adjust their behavior. In cross-cultural interactions, Japanese executives dramatically increased eye contact, increased the number of smiles, and decreased the number of aggressive persuasive tactics. The Americans were found to make a few analogous adjustments. Also, there were fewer silent periods in cross-cultural negotiations. But this is apparently not due to Japanese adjustments as much as to Americans filling potential silent periods with new arguments.

There is an important implication underlying this apparent adjustment made by the Japanese but not by the American negotiators. Anthropologists tell us that power relations usually determine who adopts and adapts behavior in cross-cultural setting. Japanese executives in an American business setting are likely to be the ones to modify their behavior. Moreover, in American negotiations status relations are less defined and less important. Japanese sellers can apparently fit into such a situation without offending American buyers.

However, if American sellers takes their normative set of bargaining behaviors to Japan, negotiations are apt to end abruptly. American sellers expect to be treated as equals and act accordingly. Japanese buyers are likely to view this rather brash behavior in lower status sellers as inappropriate and disrespectful. Japanese buyers are made to feel uncomfortable and thus, without explanation, politely shut the door to trade. American sellers do not make the first sale, and hence do not learn the Japanese system.

Given these several and substantial points of conflict in negotiation styles it seems truly remarkable that American and Japanese businesspeople ever agree on anything. It is our belief that two things have made business deals between the two largest economic powers possible. The first is the powerful reality of commercial interdependence. American and Japanese companies can, and do, achieve substantial economic benefits from cooperation. Second, businesspeople on both sides of the Pacific have learned to manage these differences in negotiation styles. The Japanese have been better at making adjustments. It is the goal of this book to help Americans improve. Thus, in the next few chapters we present a comprehensive list of instructions for Americans bargaining with Japanese executives. Included are prescriptions regarding selection of representatives, negotiation preliminaries, management of the negotiation process itself, and finally, follow-up procedures.

NOTES TO CHAPTER 3

1. Manufactured Imports Promotion Organization, *Penetrating the Japanese Market* (Tokyo, 1980), p. 16.
2. "Long Workdays," *Time*, January 12, 1981, p. 56.
3. Robert March, "Melodrama in Japanese Negotiations," *Winds* (Japan Airlines Publication Group, April 1982): 23.
4. Takeo Doi, "Some Psychological Themes in Japanese Human Relationships," in J. C. Condon and M. Saito, eds., *Intercultural Encounters in Japan* (Tokyo: Simul Press, 1974), pp. 17–26.
5. Kazuma Uyeno, *Japanese Business Glossary* (Tokyo: Mitsubishi Corporation, Toyo-keizai-Shiyosha, 1983), pp. 58–60.
6. Boye DeMente, *The Japanese Way of Doing Business* (Englewood Cliffs, N.J.: Prentice-Hall, 1981).

4 NEGOTIATOR SELECTION AND TEAM ASSIGNMENT

The initial step in business negotiations is often the selection of company representatives. Negotiators come from all ranks of firms, depending on the size of the firms involved and the size and importance of the transaction. Selection of the best representative can make or break a business deal. In a recent speech at the University of Southern California, Elliot Richardson emphasized the importance of an individual representative's characteristics in negotiations. He maintained that in the five-year Law of the Sea Conference, a delegation's power was more a function of the head delegate's personality than the economic power of the represented country. More than one American company has found that sending the wrong person to handle negotiations in Japan has led to failures.

We all have our own ideas about what makes a good negotiator. Long ago, Sir Francis Bacon told us to use "bold men for expostulation, fair-spoken men for persuasion, crafty men for inquiry and observation." Today, characteristics such as persistence, extroversion, a nimble tongue, a quick wit, or an affable demeanor come to mind. Such characteristics sound good, but do they really make a difference in business negotiations? Are they effective in Japan? Based on our discussion in the previous chapter, one would conclude that what makes a good bargainer in the United States may not lead to the best bargaining outcomes with Japanese clients. So whom do we send to Japan? What personality traits should we look for in prospective representatives of our companies?

THE SCHOLARLY OPINION

Both social psychologists and professors of business administration in American universities have been involved in the investigation of negotiator traits and bargaining outcomes. However, they have attacked the problem in two different ways. Social psychologists have conducted hundreds of bargaining experiments (primarily using college students as subjects) and looked for relationships between personality traits and outcomes of negotiation games. Meanwhile, business scholars in marketing departments of several major universities have looked for relationships between personality traits of sales representatives and sales performance. Table 4-1 lists the impressive (albeit incomplete) list of personality traits examined in both contexts.

Generally, the results of these numerous studies have been disappointing. In the majority of studies conducted in psychology departments and business schools, no systematic relationships have been found between negotiator characteristics and bargaining or sales performance. One study conducted by Richard Bagozzi at the Stanford Business School revealed a negative relationship between verbal intelligence and sales performance. That is, contrary to what one might

Table 4-1.   Bargainer Characteristics.

Risk-taking propensity	Machiavellianism
Perceived focus of control	Rigidity of thinking
Cognitive complexity	Generalized self-esteem[a]
Tolerance for ambiguity	Task-specific esteem
Self-concept (positive or negative)	Extroversion/introversion[a]
Motives (need for power, affiliation, achievement)	Forcefulness
	Sociability
Generalized trust	General intelligence
Cooperativeness	Education
Authoritarianism	Experience[a]
Internationalism	Age[a]
Flexible ethics	

a. Investigated using Japanese executives as subjects.

predict, the less intelligent sales representatives achieved higher sales performance!

We at the University of Southern California (USC) School of Business have considered the influence of five bargainer characteristics—attractiveness, self-esteem, extroversion, experience, and age—on negotiation outcomes in a series of bargaining experiments using both American and Japanese business executives as participants. We too found the five bargainer characteristics to have little influence on negotiation outcomes in either country. Only interpersonal attractiveness (the degree to which people enjoy being with the bargainer) seemed to influence negotiation outcomes, and only for the American group.

Does this mean that bargainer characteristics don't matter? Can we send just anyone to represent our companies in commercial negotiations? We believe the answer is no. Managers and companies must be selective; individual negotiators can and do make a difference. Further, we believe that the numerous scholarly studies so far conducted haven't considered the most important factors.

One line of research that does offer promise was begun more than twenty years ago. In 1963, Franklin Evans reported that in a study involving 125 insurance sales representatives and some 500 prospects, the more alike the salesman and prospect, the more probable a sale.[1] Similarity on several social, economic, physical, personality, and communicational characteristics did make a difference in selling life insurance. The explanation is that similarity promotes interpersonal attraction and ease of communication, and therefore, better negotiation outcomes. Evans' work suggests that most Americans will have a difficult time in Japan because of the great disparity in cultural values and modes of communication. However, if American representatives can be found with values and personality traits similar to those of the Japanese, then perhaps better deals can be struck with companies across the Pacific.

THE EXECUTIVE OPINION

Given this lack of "scientifically" gathered information on negotiator traits, whom does the manager send to Japan? A comparison of important negotiator traits identified by surveys of businesspeople in both countries suggests some answers.

Table 4-2.   Karrass' Negotiator Traits.

Task Performance Variables

Physical stamina
Preparation and planning skill
Knowledge of product being bought
Degree of reliability and industriousness
Degree to which person strives to achieve objectives
   (dedication to job)
General problem-solving skills
Degree of individual initiative

Aggression Variables

Persistence and determination
Willingness to take somewhat above average business or career risks
Ability to perceive and exploit available power to achieve objective
Competitiveness (desire to compete and win)
Willingness to employ force, threat, or bluff to avoid being exploited
Courage
Ability to lead and control members of own team or group

Socializing Variables

Trusting temperament
Patience
Attractive personality and sense of humor (degree to which people
   enjoy being with person)
Integrity
Tact and discretion
Fairness and open-mindedness (tolerance of other viewpoints)
Appearance
Compromising temperament

Communication Variables

Ability to express thoughts verbally
Ability to create close personal rapport with opponent
   (prior to and during negotiations)
Listening skill
Skill in communicating by signs, gestures, and silence
   (nonverbal language)
Debating ability (skill in parrying questions and answers across the table)
Skill in communicating and coordinating various objectives within
   own organization
Ability to skillfully act out a variety of negotiating roles or postures

Table 4-2. continued

Self-Worth Variables

   Ability to win respect and confidence of opponent
   Degree of self-confidence and self-esteem (personal sense of security
   Personal dignity (as differentiated from dignity of position)
   Ability to win respect and confidence of boss
   Standard of business ethics
   Status or rank in organization
   Self-control
   Willingness to risk being disliked

Thought Process Variables

   Previous negotiating experience
   Judgment and general intelligence
   Broad perspective or viewpoint
   Insight into hidden needs and reactions of own and opponent's
      organization
   Decisiveness
   Analytical ability
   Ability to think clearly and rapidly under pressure and uncertainty
   Formal education level

Source: Chester A. Karrass, *The Negotiating Game* (New York: Crowell, 1970).

In a revealing study funded by Hughes Aircraft Company in Los Angeles, Chester Karrass asked for more than 100 experienced businesspeople to choose the most important negotiator characteristics from a list of forty-five. All forty-five traits are listed in Table 4-2, and the seven most important, according to Karrass' calculations, are ranked in Table 4-3. However, we do not consider the order to be important.

At USC we have replicated Karrass' study using fifty executives from each of three countries (Japan, Brazil, and the Republic of China) as participants. The most important negotiator traits identified by each cultural group are also listed in Table 4-3. Comparison of the four lists suggests some interesting implications. The lists of the American and Brazilian executives are almost identical. Moreover, the Chinese list is closer to the Western lists (three traits in common) than to the Japanese (one trait in common). Assuming that these lists of traits reflect national negotiation styles, we can

Table 4-3. The Most Important Bargainer Characteristics According to Various Managers.

American Managers	Japanese Managers	Brazilian Managers	Chinese Managers
1. Preparation and planning skill	1. Dedication to job	1. Preparation and planning skill	1. Persistence and determination
2. Thinking under pressure	2. Perceive and exploit power	2. Thinking under pressure	2. Win respect and confidence
3. Judgment and intelligence	3. Win respect and confidence	3. Judgment and intelligence	3. Preparation and planning skill
4. Verbal expression	4. Integrity	4. Verbal expression	4. Product knowledge
5. Product knowledge	5. Listening skill	5. Product knowledge	5. Attractiveness
6. Perceive and exploit power	6. Broad perspective	6. Perceive and exploit power	6. Judgment and intelligence
7. Integrity	7. Verbal expression	7. Competitiveness	

Source: Adapted from Chester A. Karrass, *The Negotiating Game* (New York: Crowell, 1970).

see how different the Japanese bargaining style is from that of the Chinese.

Turning to the key comparison—the Japanese with the American—we find, as with all cross-cultural comparisons, similarities and differences. American and Japanese executives agree that preparation and planning skill, ability to perceive and exploit power, and integrity are important negotiator traits. But the differences in the two lists suggest important implications for the selection of negotiators to participate in cross-cultural transactions. The four remaining traits on the American list might be summarized as rational abilities—planning, thinking, intelligence, and knowledge. Alternatively, the four remaining traits on the Japanese list might be roughly classified as interpersonal skills—dedication, respect, listening skill, and broad perspective. Indeed, these differences are entirely consistent with our earlier comments regarding Japanese and American negotiation styles—the former emphasizing relationships and the latter emphasizing information about the deal.

KEY BARGAINER CHARACTERISTICS

So, whom do we send to Japan? The behavioral scientists have little to say about it. The summary opinions of our small samples of executives provide more insight, but they certainly are not the last word. Our work, based on our reading of the literature on negotiation, our management laboratory observations, our interviews with experienced bargainers, and our own experiences as negotiators in Japanese-American business transactions, suggests seven bargainer characteristics as particularly important in Japanese negotiations. They are:

1. Listening ability;
2. Interpersonal orientation;
3. Willingness to use team assistance;
4. Self-esteem;
5. High aspirations;
6. Attractiveness; and
7. Influence at headquarters.

Representatives with these qualities should be sought to fill temporary or more permanent positions in other countries. Other favorable characteristics such as those identified by American executives in Table 4–3—thinking under pressure, product knowledge, verbal expression, and so on—are of secondary importance. The seven key bargainer characteristics and the reasons for their importance are further described below.

Listening Ability

The ability to listen is crucial in any bargaining context. Negotiation is by definition joint decisionmaking. And decisions should be made with as much information as possible, including information about the clients' or partner's needs and preferences. In order to achieve the most favorable bargaining solution for both sides, bargainers must be vigilant for all the subtle indications of clients' real interests. Also, good listening is the initial step in persuasion. Before trying to change the minds of those across the bargaining table, it is best to determine, through good questions and attentive listening, what the other side needs to know. There is little point in extolling the virtues of one's product when one's potential customer already believes it is the best available or when quick delivery is foremost in his or her mind. Finally, in international transactions one's listening abilities are put to the most difficult test—ascertaining meaning in the context of less than fluent English and different nonverbal vocabularies.

Interpersonal Orientation

This characteristic includes two aspects. First, bargainers must attend to a client's or supplier's behavior; second, they must respond accordingly. Successful bargainers who have high interpersonal orientations adjust their bargaining approach according to the situation and the behavior of their bargaining partners. When clients take a competitive approach, bargainers behave competitively. When clients are cooperative, bargainers respond in kind. Because negotiation styles differ from country to country (and person to person) taking a flexible approach to negotiations, or "playing the chameleon," is important.

Willingness to Use Team Assistance

This trait can make a substantial difference in international business negotiations. Expertise in technical details, financial matters, cultural considerations, and the all-important maintenance of business relationships is simply too much to expect of one person—even an American executive! Application engineers, financial analysts, interpreters, and foreign agents should be included and used when appropriate. The additional expense may be an important investment. Also, observation of negotiations can be a valuable training experience for younger members of an organization. Even if they add little to the discussion, their presence may make a difference. We feel that more important than the "product knowledge" mentioned by the American executives in Table 4–3 is the personal quality of being able to use product experts. This is particularly true in many places in the world where establishing personal relationships is more important than quick information.

Self-esteem

The job of representatives is one of the most difficult of all. Bridging the gap between companies and cultures can be exhausting work. Negotiations are being conducted not only with clients but also with the home office. Clients question your company's policies. Sales managers question the time you invest in building personal relationships, and so on. Self-esteem, or belief in one's own ideas, will be an important personal asset for those working in such situations of role ambiguity.

High Aspirations

High expectations regarding the business deal are key. One of the basic lessons of the hundreds of bargaining studies mentioned earlier is that bargainers who ask for more in the beginning end up getting more. Thus, given two otherwise equal executives, the one with higher aspirations is the better one to send.

Attractiveness

By attractiveness we don't mean good looks but rather personal qualities that make the social contact enjoyable. We mentioned the importance of personal relationships in business negotiations, and such transactions are very much a social activity. Interpersonal attraction not only smooths the social contact points but also tends to encourage the flow of information from the other side of the table. Thus better, more informed decisions can be made regarding the business deal.

Influence at Headquarters

This characteristic will be particularly important in international negotiations. We mentioned above the difficulty of the international representative's job—bridging both organizational and cultural barriers. Many representatives we have interviewed suggest that the toughest part of business negotiations is selling the agreement to headquarters. Moreover, there is danger in presenting the other side's point of view too well—your own management might trust you less. In choosing a representative for negotiations in a foreign country, influence at headquarters will be a criterion worth much consideration.

Personnel decisions regarding negotiations with Japanese firms therefore deserve special attention. We must add to the list of desirable characteristics. Patience will be critical in Japan. Negotiations and decisions take longer—particularly the early stages of nontask sounding and information exchanges. Also, quiet men and women should be sent to Japan. We don't mean introverts. Rather, by quiet we mean individuals who are good listeners and are comfortable with silence.

A final concern is ethnocentrism. We all suffer from this to a degree. But even those with the broadest view will be put to the test in Japan. Individuals harboring chauvinstic cultural attitudes will almost always do poorly in Japan, where mutual respect anchors all interpersonal contact.

SELECTING THE TEAM

Now that we know what we're looking for in a negotiator to send to Japan, how do we measure these important personality traits? We have four options. First, the most frequently used personnel selection device is the interview. Prospective representatives might be asked to assess their own characteristics, and some factors may actually be measured during the interview—listening ability for example. Second, paper and pencil psychological tests are often used in employment and assignment decisions. However, we feel this approach is the least useful. Third, observation of the various characteristics during actual business negotiations is perhaps the best measure. Fourth, when field observations are not possible, as with new employees, role playing and observation are the next best methods of measuring personality traits and predicting future performance.

The next considerations are how many negotiators to send and what levels of management are appropriate? The "I-can-go-it-alone" style of American bargainers suggests sending one negotiator (usually middle management) with authority to sign. However, decisions regarding negotiation team composition must be made with consideration of the Japanese side.

A business negotiation team in Japan typically consists of the five following roles or positions:

1. *Shokai-sha* (introducer);
2. *Sutaffu* (operational staff);
3. *Kacho/Bucho* (middle managers);
4. *Shacho* (chief executive officer); and, if necessary,
5. *Chukai-sha* (mediator).

Shokai-Sha

The *shokai-sha*—literally, the person who introduces—is a neutral third party who makes initial contact with the courted party in a business deal in Japan. This third-party introduction is absolutely necessary. The *shokai-sha* will ordinarily participate in the business discussion during the initial meeting (and perhaps the second one) and the last meeting, when the chief executives meet to give final, ceremonial approval to the deal. *Shokai-sha* may also help locate interpreters when necessary. For an American company courting a Japanese company, finding and using the appropriate *shokai-sha* is essential. An American firm being approached by a Japanese company will always be contacted initially by the *shokai-sha.*

There are four kinds of institutions in the United States that can provide *shokai-sha* services and appropriate personnel. They are (1) Japanese trading companies, (2) Japanese banks, (3) American law firms, and (4) American accounting firms. All provide excellent services, but each has special associated considerations.

Both Japanese trading companies and banks will be able to arrange introductions with only a limited group of Japanese companies—those in their "family" of companies. For example, Mitsubishi Trading Company or Mitsubishi Bank would not be appropriate *shokai-sha* for Hitachi, Inc., but would be appropriate for Mitsubishi Electronics, Ltd. If an American company wishes to determine which bank or trading company is appropriate, the Japan Company Book (*Kaisha Shikiho*), available at JETRO and Japanese consulate offices, should be consulted (Exhibit 4-1). Usually, the costs of the *shokai-sha* services will be cheaper for banks than trading companies. That is, purchase of associated financial services when banks act as *shokai-sha*, is usually less expensive than the commissions and other "pieces of the action" when trading companies are involved.

American law firms and major accounting firms with Japanese practice divisions can also provide excellent *shokai-sha* services. The commissions associated with the former are generally higher but may be appropriate when substantial legal review is necessary. Major international banks with substantial operations in Japan may also provide *shokai-sha* services.

Finally, it should be noted that frequently two kinds of *shokai-sha* may be appropriate. That is, it may be best for operational level personnel of the *shokai-sha* firm to introduce operational level personnel of the two courting firms. And at the same time, the president of the *shokai-sha* firm should introduce the top executive officers.

Sutaffu

Once the proper introductions have been made, the work begins in earnest. *Sutaffu*, or operational level staff (personnel involved with

Exhibit 4-1. Japanese Company Book (*Kaisha Shikiho*): An Excerpt.

NISSAN MOTOR

7201 Con. 22
日産自動車

Est.: December,1933   **Listing Date:** January,1951
Head Office: 6-17-1, Ginza, Chuoku, Tokyo 104
Tel.: 03-543-5523   **Telex:** 22503
Head Office: 2, Takaracho, Kanagawaku, Yokohama 221
Factory(ies): Oppama, Zama, Tochigi, Murayama, Yokohama & others
Chairman: Katsuji Kawamata   **President:** Takashi Ishihara
References: Industrial Bank, Fuji, Sumitomo, Kyowa, Yasuda Trust
Listed: Tokyo, Osaka, Nagoya, Kyoto, Fukuoka, Niigata, Sapporo, FRA
Underwriters: Yamaichi, Nikko, Daiwa, Wako, New Japan

Capital Change	Allotment Ratio	Capital (¥ mil.)
May '78	PO50¥765	69,052
Sep. '78	1:10G	75,995
Nov. '80	EDR50¥689	79,413
May '81	EDR60¥797	82,802
Sep. '83	1:10G	99,738
*1st '84	1:20G	
Mar. '83	©SF100m.	¥700
Mar. '83	©$100m.	¥700
Mar. '83	©SF100m.	¥700

Capital: (¥50 par value)	86,414	
(¥mil.)	• Sep. '83	• Sep. '82
Total Assets:	2,308,257	2,181,129
Stockholders' Equity:	1,058,553	979,189
Equity Ratio (%):	45.9	44.9
Capital Surplus:	200,485	196,114
Debts:	303,969	271,710
Interest & Dividend Net:	30,653	25,161
Employees (Age): (Sep.'83)	60,819(35)	
No.of Stockholders: (Sep.'83)	53,670	
No.of Shares Out.: (1000 shares)	1,709,689	

Major Stockholders: (1000 shares)		(%)
Industrial Bank of Japan	106,136	(6.2)
Swiss Credit Bank Zurich	94,813	(5.5)
Dai-ichi Mutual Life Ins.	88,588	(5.2)
Fuji Bank	83,439	(4.9)
Nippon Life Ins.	66,904	(3.9)
Sumitomo Bank	51,119	(3.0)
Kyowa Bank	46,293	(2.7)
Yasuda Trust & Banking	42,412	(2.5)
Nissan F.& M.Ins.	38,627	(2.3)
Foreign Ownership	137,431	(8.0)

Sales Breakdown (%, Sep.)	• '83	• '82	• '81
Automobiles	86	86	87
KD sets	2	1	2
Auto parts & others	12	13	11
Export Ratio	56	55	53
Highest in CP (¥mil.)	Mar.'80	183,016	

Business Results: (¥mil.; ¥)

	Sales	Operating Profit	Current Profit	Net Profit	Earnings P.S.	Dividend P.S.	Equity P.S.
Mar.1980	2,738,868	153,585	183,016	87,457	57.1	12	449.2
Mar.1981	3,016,190	124,458	166,070	85,911	53.9	13	499.3
Mar.1982	3,198,724	134,340	178,569	86,068	50.8	14	553.3
Mar.1983	3,187,722	102,124	154,347	95,477	56.1	14	605.3
Mar.1984*	3,430,000	70,000	124,000	70,000	37.0	14~15	
Mar.1985*	3,600,000	110,000	160,000	80,000	42.2	14~15	
·Sep. 1981	1,621,991	75,950	95,372	42,118	24.9	7	534.0
·Sep. 1982	1,642,826	65,651	92,367	49,536	29.1	7	576.0
·Sep. 1983	1,683,656	29,067	61,106	35,957	21.0	7	619.1

Characteristics: 2nd-ranked auto manufacturer in Japan. Active in overseas production, incl. small trucks in US. Succeeded in test operating "H-1 rocket" engine. Noted for excellent aerospace technologies.
Remarks: New models pushing sales up 3% to 2.53 mil units. Share of high-grade cars increasing but export profitability worsening due to high yen rate. Increased support for sales firms and depreciation depress profit. US small-truck plant operating smoothly, studying passenger car production. Overseas loan and investment balance exceeds ¥200 bil. Decided to make advance into UK. 50th anniversary special dividend and gratis issue possible.

the prospective deal on a day-to-day basis), meet to exchange information and hammer out concessions and agreements. Such meetings may occur frequently and over a long period of time until both sides are satisfied with the outcome.

Kacho/Bucho

The *Kacho/Bucho*, or middle managers, may attend operational staff level meetings but will seldom participate in the discussions and persuasive efforts. Occasionally, the middle managers will confirm concessions and decisions made during the other meetings. However, they will seldom make decisions at the negotiation table. Their function is to listen and observe, not to persuade or decide.

Shacho

The *Shacho*, or chief executives, act as ceremonial figures in Japanese negotiations. Ordinarily, they will be brought in at the final signing of the agreement. They are not involved in the discussions of details, *nor do they make the decisions.* Most importantly, chief executives of Japanese firms are not persuaded. Recall the previous description of the consensus decisionmaking in Japanese organizations. Not only are persuasive tactics ineffective with top Japanese executives, they are considered boorish behavior.

Top Japanese executives may be included in initial meetings or at an intermediate stage to communicate the importance of the deal. But in neither case do they participate in substantive business talks. They have neither the knowledge of details nor the willingness to make a decision without consultation.

Chukai-Sha

The final participant or role to be played on a Japanese negotiation team is that of *chukai-sha*, or mediator. The job of the third party *chukai-sha* is to settle disputes between the two negotiating companies. Rather than making threats and using other aggressive persuasive appeals, stalemated negotiators call in a *chukai-sha* when an impasse is reached.

The American style of negotiation is much different. The formality and ceremony, the tight constraints of the well-defined roles, and the extra cost of third parties all seem like so much nonsense from the American perspective. But the best deal (and sometimes the only deal) will be made when American negotiation teams are assembled with full consideration given to the Japanese team's composition, roles, and bargaining process.

The first rule of negotiation team composition is to remember that in Japan talk flows horizontally across levels, not vertically between levels. Also, what is talked about varies from level to level. That is, when top executives are present, they talk to corresponding top executives about primarily non-task-related matters. Executives at other levels may be asked questions (with short answers expected), but the focus of such meetings is the development of personal relations at the top level. When only middle managers and operational staff are present, middle managers confirm decisions and commitments to corresponding middle managers. Or, middle managers listen while operational staff members exchange information and try to persuade one another. Given these circumstances, it is our recommendation that an American negotiation team should reflect the composition and behaviors of the Japanese team.

It should be noted that it is possible, when the Japanese firm is doing the courting, for an American middle manager to handle more than one role. Often, American managers pride themselves in having detailed information as well as decisionmaking authority. But a lone American negotiator will accomplish the most when he or she plays the appropriate role at the appropriate time. That is, persuasive tactics should be directed toward the Japanese operational staff. Only middle managers on the Japanese side should be expected to make commitments, and then only after separate consultation with their operational staff. And when the top Japanese executive is present, task-related discussions are completely inappropriate and ineffective. American negotiators can get by using such a single-handed approach, but the better strategy is to include and use the three levels of executives in a well planned and coordinated team effort with each executive playing the proper role.

There are two other important but more subtle reasons for including more than one American when bargaining in Japan. First, the image of the American negotiator is boosted if an assistant accompanies him or her to handle minor details. Second, it will almost always be to the American's advantage to establish an informal channel of

---

Exhibit 4-2. The Devil's Tongue: Misunderstandings Can Create Both Obstacles and Insulation.

The first person pronoun "I" is a basic starting point: *ego, je, ich, io, ya.* In Japanese, where nothing is that simple, the word has two dozen or more forms, depending on who is talking, and to whom, and the social relationship between them. An elderly man might refer to himself as *washi,* but his wife would say *watashi,* or, for that matter, *atakushi,* or *atashi;* their daughter might say *atai* and their son *boku.* Then there is *temae,* which means both "you" and "I." But the Japanese often evade these social difficulties by dropping all pronouns entirely.

The "devils language" is the description generally attributed to St. Francis Xavier, the sixteenth century Jesuit missionary. Others have seen in the intricacies of the language a major influence on Japan's intellectual and artistic styles, even on its basic national character. Yet, sympathetic observers also believe that the language may represent a serious obstacle to Japan's functioning as a world power. According to former U.S. Ambassador Edwin O. Reischauer, "Japanese ideas are transmitted abroad only very weakly and through the filter of a few foreign 'experts.' . . . Japanese intellectual life for the most part goes on behind a language barrier."

To cross that barrier, translators and interpreters are more necessary but less effective, since the Japanese language not only is difficult in itself but represents a quite different concept of speech. Anthropologist Masao Kunihiro notes: "English is intended strictly for communication. Japanese is primarily interested in feeling out the other person's mood." Misunderstandings are a constant hazard. At one top-level conference, for example, President Nixon asked for a cut in Japanese textile exports, and Prime Minister Sato answered, "Zensho shimasu," which was translated literally as "I'll handle it as well as I can." Nixon thought that meant "I'll take care of it," but the Japanese understood it to mean something like "Let's talk about something else."

"Japanese can be made vague," says Paul Anderer, who teaches Japanese literature at Columbia University, "but the language is extraordinarily precise in determining who you are as you speak to someone else about what it is that you or that other person needs."

Source: *Time,* August 1, 1983: 40.

communication between executives at lower levels. Things can and will be said by the lowest level Japanese that can't be said at the negotiation table. Such an informal channel of communication is best established using lower level executives on each side.

Our final comment regarding negotiation team selection concerns interpreters. Very few Americans speak Japanese. Thus, despite the disadvantages of using an interpreter, they are often a necessity. Particularly when substantive discussions begin, having *your own* interpreter will be important for two reasons. First, you will need to brief the interpreter before discussions begin. Second, you will need to sit with the interpreter after the negotiations end each day to assess results and the interests of the Japanese side. Without your own interpreter neither option is open to you.

The best interpreters will be a help in the negotiations not only by translating, but by communicating the meanings intended. (See Exhibit 4-2 for an idea of the difficulties of interpreting Japanese to English and vice versa.) Interpreters can hurt or help you, and generally you get what you pay for. Their fees vary depending on the level of technical knowledge and competence you require. It is safe to budget $100 to $150 per half day. Interpreters should be briefed on the background and terminology of the deal but not necessarily on your strategies. It must be remembered that interpreters are third parties. Even though they are paid by you they have different, personal motives.

The *shokai-sha* is perhaps the best source of information about selecting interpreters. Additionally, business information centers, listed in the Appendix, can provide references to the interpreters and interpreting companies. References such as the Japanese Yellow Pages also list major interpreting companies.

CONCLUSIONS

By nature Americans prefer to "go it alone" in a business negotiation. However, even in the United States this is often not the best practice. There is much to be gained by a team approach. Listening, debating, maintaining personal relationships, making calculations, and keeping track of technical information are all required at the negotiation table. Coordinated teamwork can accomplish such tasks more efficiently. And finally, there is the added social pressure of numbers—a simple and subtle consideration but an important one.

When meeting with Japanese clients, teamwork will be doubly important. Because the Japanese divide the labor of negotiation into clearly specified roles and functions, American negotiators will have to adjust their approach. This is particularly so when Americans travel to Japan. Finally, the individuals chosen to bargain with Japanese clients should have special characteristics—good listening skills, interpersonal orientation, patience, a broad world view, and so forth. Teams and negotiators should be picked carefully for dealing with Japanese clients and partners. Selection decisions can easily make or break a trans-Pacific business relationship.

NOTES TO CHAPTER 4

1. Franklin B. Evans, "Selling as a Dyadic Relationship," *American Behavioral Scientist*, 6 (May 1963): 76–79.

5 NEGOTIATION PRELIMINARIES

Once the best negotiation team has been selected it is time to prepare for the meetings. These preparations include two aspects. First, gathering information and planning strategies and tactics will be important. Second, manipulation of the negotiation situation may have a dramatic impact on the negotiation process and outcomes. The best negotiators on both sides of the Pacific manage such details with great care. To get the most out of business negotiations it is important to have every causal factor working in your favor. The time spent in careful planning and detailed adjustment of situational factors is an important investment.

EFFICIENT PREPARATIONS

Any experienced business negotiator will tell you that there's never enough time to get ready. Given the typical time constraints of international negotiations, preparations must be accomplished efficiently. The homework must be done before bargaining begins. Toward the goal of efficiency in preparation and planning for bargaining with Japanese clients, we provide the following checklist:

1. Assessment of the situation and the people;
2. Facts to confirm during the negotiation;

51

3. Agenda;
4. Best alternative to a negotiation agreement (BATNA);
5. Concession strategies; and
6. Team assignments.

Assessment of the Situation and the People

It is only common sense to learn as much as possible about a potential client or partner before negotiations begin. All kinds of information might be pertinent depending on the nature of the contemplated deal. Various sorts of financial data and competitive information regarding American companies are available to other American firms. Much the same information is available about Japanese firms. For example, one can find distribution partners, *shokai-sha*, and financial and marketing data. In the Appendix we include a guide to the various sources of financial and marketing information in Japan. The first step in preparing for many such negotiations is mining the critical information from several resources.

The most illuminating of these resources are the Japanese "Who's Who" books, *Jinji Koshinroku* and *Zen Nippon Shinshiroku* (Exhibit 5-1). These volumes contain broad biographical data about the top executives in many publicly and privately held firms in Japan. Given the crucial nature of nontask sounding in Japanese business negotiations, knowledge of a particular executive's background, hobbies, and family status can be an enormous advantage.

It should be clearly understood that knowing who you will be bargaining with in Japan is far more important than most Americans would assume. If you and your business associates step off the plane with no personal or professional perspectives on your Japanese counterparts, you can expect little success once the meetings begin.

In addition to the public sources of information about Japanese companies and executives, informal sources should be consulted. Other American companies that have dealt with the courted Japanese firm might be valuable sources of information. A final source of information specific to the prospective deal will be the *shokai-sha*.

The last step is sizing up the probable goals and preferences of the Japanese side of analysis of the various data using a Japanese perspective rather than an American one. In acquisitions, the Japanese tendency to focus on asset evaluations rather than potential cash flow

---

Exhibit 5-1.   A Translated Page from the Shinshiroku.

- TOSHIO SANO, President Kyokuto Note Company

- Born   Osaka Prefecture
  Residence   Osaka City
  Mother   Harue, born 1908
  Wife   Hiroko, born 1929
  1st son   Takatoshi, born 1950
  1st daughter Taeko, born 1952
  2nd son   Masatoshi, born 1954
  2nd daughter Emiko, born 1956

- Born first son of Harukichi in Kyoto on September 5, 1925

- Graduated from Doshisha Engineering School (now University) and joined Sano Note Company in 1947

- Company was renamed as Kyokuto Note and he became president in 1958

- He became statutory auditor of Kyokuto Stationery Company in 1957

- 1959—received a governmental award

- Hobbies—photography, reading books, golf

- Religion—Tenrikyo

- Address—117 Matsugahana-cho Tennoji-ku
          Osaka City, JAPAN T543

- Home telephone—06-771-2313

---

streams, as is typical in America, and the often mentioned emphasis on long-term, gradual growth are Japanese modes of business reasoning that should be kept in mind. A comparison of automobile production in the United States and in Japan is most revealing of the difference in perspectives (Figure 5-1). Notice the volatility in American production versus the slow, steady growth of Japanese production. These figures reflect the basic view of Japanese business executives. As described in detail by Ouchi in *Theory Z* and Pascale and Athos in *The Art of Japanese Management*, the Japanese side will most likely be looking for stable growth over at least a ten-year period. Meanwhile, American companies and executives, looking at the same information, would be focusing on length of payback and profits in the first three years.

Figure 5-1. Japanese and U.S. Motor Vehicle Production.

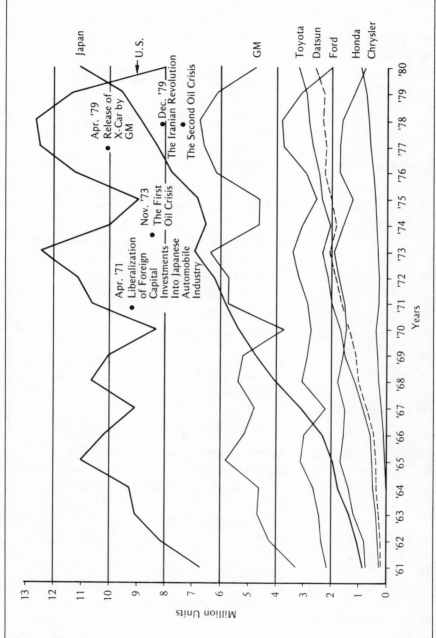

Source: Japan Automobile Manufacturers' Association, "Automobile Monthly Statistic Report" (Tokyo: Japan Automobile Manufacturers' Association, January 1981).

Once the file on the Japanese company is complete, it is time to evaluate carefully your own company's situation. The kind of economic analysis you have undertaken regarding the Japanese should be replicated regarding your own company. Without question the Japanese side will do the same, and you need to anticipate what they know about you. Finally, your own instructions from top management and your authority limits should be clearly understood. This latter aspect of preparations is often taken for granted, and lack of attention to this detail can cause serious problems during and after the negotiations. Frequently, American managers in the heat of a long negotiation will overstep their authority and make commitments that later must be retracted. "I'll take full responsibility," runs the cliche.

Facts to Confirm During the Negotiation

No matter how careful the analysis and how complete the information available, all critical information and assumptions should be reconfirmed at the negotiation table. As part of the preparations a list of such facts should be discussed among the members of the negotiation team, and specific questions should be written down. We have found again and again that surprises (both pleasant and unpleasant) often surface as part of this confirmation of facts. For example, a Japanese client was recently considering the purchase of a California independent bank. As part of the preparations for negotiations the Japanese consulted past annual reports and the Findley Report, which rates the performance of independent banks in the state. The potential acquisition had a history of excellent performance—a "premier" rating for the previous five years. On the surface, things looked good. However, at the negotiation table, a different picture came to light. It so happened that the comptroller of currency had recently assigned the bank a "troubled" status.

Agenda

Most business negotiators come to the negotiation table with an agenda for the meeting in mind. We feel it is important to do two things with that agenda. First, write out the agenda for all members of your negotiating team. Second, don't try to settle each issue one at a time. This latter recommendation goes against the grain of the typical American sequential approach. However, in any bargaining situation it is better to get all the issues and interests out on the table before trying to settle any one of them. This will be particularly true when the other side consists of representatives from a Japanese company.

You should understand that the Japanese bargainers will also bring with them a carefully considered agenda, and you may end up bargaining over agendas. The tendency will be for the Japanese side to be more flexible toward setting the order of topics but much less flexible about the choice of topics.

A Japanese agenda permits skipping around among selected topics. A safe strategy for the American side is to check beforehand with Japanese operational level people about the agenda. However, there can be some value in surprise. We have witnessed American bargainers scrapping a previously agreed upon agenda, making the Japanese side scramble, and thus creating a major distraction, giving the American side time to regroup thoughts and strategies. However, this tactic should be used with caution as it will result in great discomfort for the Japanese.

The Best Alternative to Negotiated Agreement

Fisher and Ury, in their popular book, *Getting To Yes*, point out that an often skipped crucial aspect of negotiation preparations is a clear definition of the best alternative to a negotiated agreement, or BATNA. They suggest, and we agree, that negotiators and managers must spend time considering what happens next if the deal doesn't work out. "Is there another Japanese firm to court or should we just concentrate on our domestic business for now and try again later?" The BATNA sets the cut-off point where negotiations no longer make sense. But it is more than a simple bottom line; it is a kind of contingency plan.

Concession Strategies

Concession strategies should be decided upon and written down before negotiations begin. Such a process—discussion and recording—

goes a long way toward ensuring that negotiators stick to the strategies. In the midst of a long negotiation there is a tendency to make what we call "streaks" of concessions. The only way we have found to avoid this is careful planning and commitment before negotiation begins.

Of particular concern is the American propensity to "split the difference." Never split the difference! Have specific reasons for the size of each concession you make.

Finally, you will notice very quickly that Japanese bargainers never make a concession without first taking a break. Issues and arguments are reconsidered away from the social pressure of the negotiation table. This is a good practice for Americans to emulate.

Team Assignments

The final step in negotiation planning is role assignments. We mentioned earlier the importance of the different roles in Japanese bargaining. Each American bargainer should understand his or her corresponding role. Other kinds of team assignments might include listening responsibilities, monitoring the agenda, or concession strategies. And perhaps roles should be adjusted to circumstances or over time.

MANIPULATION OF THE NEGOTIATION SITUATION

The second aspect of negotiation preliminaries is manipulation of the negotiation situation to your company's advantage. Some of the issues we raise in this section may appear trivial, but the most skilled negotiators and your Japanese clients always consider them. Particularly in a tough negotiation, everything should be working in your favor. If situational factors are working against you, it will be important before the negotiations begin to manipulate them. Also, management of situational factors may be important once the discussions have commenced. In the pages to follow we will consider seven situational factors that we consider particularly important. They are:

1. Location;
2. Physical arrangements;

3. Number of parties;
4. Number of participants;
5. Audiences (news media, etc.);
6. Communications channels; and
7. Time limits.

All seven factors are ordinarily set before negotiations begin. All can and should be manipulated to your advantage. Any one can make the difference between success and failure in business negotiations with executives from Japan.

Location

The location of the negotiations is perhaps the most important situational factor for several reasons, both practical and psychological. Having the "home court" is an advantage because the home team has all its information resources readily available and all the necessary team members close by. Alternatively, the traveling team brings the minimum necessary resources, information, and players, and it stays in hotels. But perhaps a greater advantage the home team enjoys is psychological—a perception of power. If the other side is coming to you, that means you have something they want. You are in control of the scarce resource, whether it be a product (you're the seller) or access to a key market (you're the buyer). Smart negotiators will always try to hold negotiations in their own offices. Short of this, a neutral location is best.

The location factor will be even more important when dealing with Japanese clients or partners, for it communicates power much louder in Japan. Thus, in business dealings between Japanese we see a strong emphasis on getting to a neutral location, such as a restaurant or bar.

Let us assume that your Japanese clients and prospective partners play the cordial host and invite you to Japan. They may call on you initially in the United States to "bait the hook." However, they will be careful to mention that the visit to your offices was just incidental to other business. After such initial contact, you may be invited to Japan. "Kyoto is lovely this time of year, and while you're on the trip you might stop by our factory. "The Japanese side will be very careful to manipulate the negotiation setting to their advantage. If you are clearly in the weaker position (that is, fewer alternatives to making the deal), then it will be best to go to Japan. But where power relations are more equal, the best response to a Japanese invitation is a counter invitation for their executives to visit the United States and your offices. A simple refusal to go to Japan would be inappropriate. Instead, a "come-see-Lake-Michigan" approach is recommended. You may end up bargaining over location; however, this bargaining is best handled in a subtle and indirect manner.

In the event that neither side gives in to the other's suggestions, then it's time to suggest that negotiations be held in a neutral location such as Hawaii. It's not just the golf courses and beaches that explain why so many trans-Pacific business deals are struck at the Kahala Hilton. This neutral location, equally convenient to both parties and indicative of equal power relations, provides a place where both sides are subject to the same expenses, information, and time constraints. Both sides communicate, albeit subtly, that they have alternatives to bargaining; they don't *have to* travel to Japan, or *have to* travel to the United States. On the other hand, each side is confirming the other side's power by not holding out for a home court advantage.

In the event that you choose to travel to Japan, there are some things that can be done to reduce the Japanese home court advantage. One is to make arrangements for meeting facilities at your hotel (or your bank, or a subsidiary's office) and invite the Japanese executives to call on you. You might argue, "I've already made the arrangements and everything is all set," or perhaps you need to wait for an important phone call. This may not help much, but it may help some.

One final comment must be made about location of negotiations. Although restaurants, bars, and golf courses are all important locations for bargaining in Japan, the kinds of bargaining behaviors appropriate is these settings are very much limited. Generally, in these informal settings almost all talk is nontask sounding. One Japanese executive suggested that 98 percent of the conversation has to do with sports, politics, and family, while only 2 percent deals with business. Usually, the task-related matters are discussed indirectly, very briefly, and toward the end of the evening, after a few drinks.

For example, recently Peter Magowan, CEO and chairman of the board of Safeway Stores, Inc., and his associates were visiting Japan to meet with his Japanese partners' companies and negotiate an increased level of import-export business. The day after their arrival in Tokyo, they visited retail stores with which they deal. Later, Magowan and his associates graciously accepted the Japanese negotiator's invitation to dinner at a plush Japanese restaurant overlooking the beautiful garden of the Hotel New Otani in Tokyo. Dinner was elaborate, including more than fifteen dishes with the flavor of spring. At the end of dinner the chef brought in a huge birthday cake to celebrate Magowan's fortieth birthday. All of the Japanese businessmen sang a happy birthday song in Japanese. Blowing out of the candles and gift giving marked the end of the evening. As all the members were ushered toward the exit, one negotiator pulled his American counterpart to the side and whispered the amount of exports and imports the Japanese were willing to approve.

Physical Arrangements

Once the negotiation site has been agreed upon, then comes the question of specific physical arrangements. American bargainers should understand that the physical arrangements of the bargaining room will be much more important and will communicate far more to Japanese executives. Americans value and feel comfortable with informality. Japanese value and feel comfortable with formality. If you travel to Japan, the Japanese will manage the physical arrangements of the negotiations (that is, unless you make the arrangements). The formal seating arrangement by rank is modeled in Figure 5-2. The only advice we have for Americans in such situations is to ask the Japanese where to sit. They will have a specific arrangement in mind, and if you ignore their arrangement they will feel uncomfortable.

If the Japanese are calling at your offices, then we recommend setting the physical arrangements to make them feel comfortable and more cooperative. If you wish to communicate that you are interested in the prospective business deal, then the most appropriate atmosphere will be a comfortable living room setting without desks or conference tables. Many chief executives have such furnishings in their offices, and for more reasons than one, a brief nontask encounter with the American CEO may be the appropriate first step. For

Figure 5-2. Seating Arrangement at the Aisatsu.

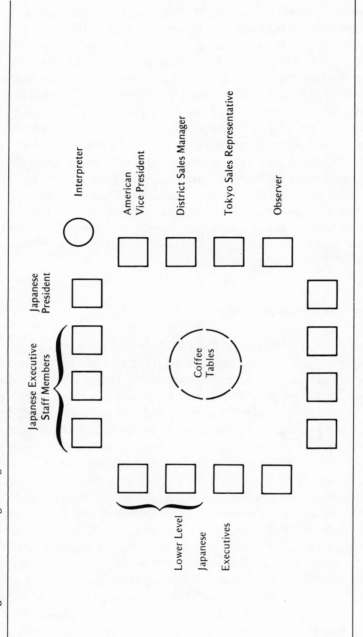

companies that have frequent visits by Japanese clients, a specific room should be set aside and furnished as described.

Given that you wish to greet the Japanese visitors as honored guests, they should also be seated appropriately. But what is the "best seat in the house" to an American may not be the best seat from the Japanese perspective. Two criteria are important to the Japanese: (1) distance from the door and (2) location of the center of focus in the room. The top Japanese executive will feel most comfortable seated furthest from the door and framed by the focal object, which is usually a window with a view or a large painting. In most American meeting rooms these criteria are complementary; the focal point is furthest from the door. This is also done at dinners and other business-related functions. We recommend place cards as an easy way to avoid a faux pas. Finally, if a couch is in the room, it will be best to sit the Japanese client there, by himself, because size of the chair is another signal of status.

Number of Parties

In many trans-Pacific business deals, more than two companies are involved. Often, in addition to a buyer and a seller there are other involved suppliers, engineering consulting firms, banks, trading companies, and government offices. For example, in the recent Toyota–GM joint venture talks, not only was the general trading firm that acted as *Shokai-sha* involved but also the United Auto Workers, the Federal Trade Commission, and numerous other local governmental bodies. Another example is that of Safeway investment in Allied Import Company (AIC), where six parties were involved in the contract signing ceremony: Safeway, AIC, and four of the AIC member companies. Generally, the more parties involved, the more complex and more difficult the negotiations. Despite such common sense, our American impatience often leads us to try to get everyone together and hammer out an agreement. Such attempts almost always end in frustration. It is our recommendation that negotiations include as few parties as possible—hopefully just representatives of the two primary companies. If more than one other party is involved we recommend a *nemawashi* approach which includes meeting with the separate parties individually and calling everyone together only for the formality of signing.

Occasionally, there may be some benefit to meeting with all parties in the early stages—as when everyone except the client agrees with you. But such circumstances will be rare, particularly when other Japanese companies are involved. You should be aware that Japanese companies will try to use this approach. In response you should always ask who is going to be involved and why. If you feel the reason is insufficient, you might suggest that things may be "simpler" without them. Alternatively, if you plan to bring along a third party, you should let the Japanese know ahead of time and be prepared with a good explanation.

Number of Participants

In negotiations, Americans are almost always outnumbered by Japanese. We consider this to be a serious disadvantage. In the previous chapter we mentioned the importance of finding out whom the other side is sending and then putting your team together in response. Moreover, you shouldn't hesitate to include additional members on your team such as financial or technical experts. The extra expense may be a wise investment.

You should also appreciate how important numbers are to your Japanese counterparts. They will bring along technical specialists and younger nonparticipants for on-the-job training. They will make one person responsible for carefully observing your nonverbal and verbal responses to their proposals; that person's evaluation and comments will appear in a written report. Since a committee will make the decision, they will bring along a committee of deciders.

In addition to bringing along extra team members, the relative numbers can be manipulated in other, sometimes unethical, ways. We have heard of Chinese negotiators who, when faced with large numbers of visiting Japanese negotiators, purposefully delay progress. As a result some of the other side's team returns home and the difference in numbers is reduced. We don't suggest you use such tactics, but you should be aware that they may be used against you.

Finally, it is possible to include too many people on your side. One such case regarded a prospective franchise agreement between a major chain of American restaurants and a Japanese investment group. The executive vice-president and corporate counsel for the U.S. company was in charge of the American team. Because of his concern for the best contract, he included an attorney in Japan in addition to his corporate lawyer in the United States. The Japanese became concerned with the legal aspects of the negotiation and decided to hire a Japanese attorney of their own. Thus, four lawyers, including the executive vice-president, were involved. With so many legal opinions, the situation soon turned sour and the Japanese backed out of the discussions.

Audiences

In any particular business deal there might be a number of audiences that could exercise influence on the negotiation outcomes. The GM–Toyota joint venture is a case in point. Consider how many audiences exist:

1. Other suitors—Ford (jilted by Toyota in 1981), Chrysler (a current critic);
2. Governmental agencies—FTC (antitrust), Congress (trade barrier saber rattling), Commerce Department and U.S. Trade Representative, California and local municipal governments;
3. Public opinion;
4. United Auto Workers; and
5. Related competitors—Ford, Chrysler, American, Nissan, Toyota Motor-Sales USA, and GM subsidiaries.

Now consider how the two companies might manipulate these various audiences to their advantage. All the audiences have an interest and a stake in how the GM–Toyota talks continue, and all can be manipulated through selective leaking of information.

We know such manipulations do occur in deals between Japanese companies and between American companies. We are familiar with at least two cases in which information was deliberately leaked to the news media to pressure the other negotiating party to agree to the terms of the proposal. It is difficult for the other party to say no to an already publicized agreement. However, extreme caution is advised in this area. Often, the action by one party may result in mistrust and a breakdown in the negotiations. Such was the result in one of the two cases. In particular, trying to influence negotiations through leaking information to a foreign press (that is, Americans in Japan or vice versa) is fraught with danger.

You should anticipate that Japanese clients or partners may manipulate audiences for their advantage, particularly Japanese audiences with which they are more familiar. You should also be aware of audience reactions that may help you, and you should know how to elicit such reactions when appropriate.

Channels of Communication

Face-to-face negotiations with Japanese clients are always recommended. Other channels of communication that might be used for negotiations in the United States simply are not effective nor acceptable. As described earlier, the Japanese social system is built around almost continuous face-to-face contact. Too much of the important, subtly transmitted information can't be communicated in a letter, memo, telex, telephone call or even teleconferencing. Moreover, it is much harder for Japanese bargainers to say no in the face-to-face situation. The social pressure and *wa* preclude negative responses, and these pressures are not so strong over the phone or in a telex.

Time Limits

If location is not the single most important aspect of the negotiation situation, then time limits are. Generally, the side that has more time *and knows it* is in a stronger bargaining position. The side with less time is forced to make concessions in order to move the other toward agreement. The use of time can be a powerful bargaining tool.

Ordinarily, time constraints are established by factors beyond the control of negotiators. On the selling side, orders must be secured to keep the factory busy, the expenses of foreign travel are substantial, other customers must be called on, quotas must be filled, and the home office management is in a hurry. Likewise, purchasers must bargain with other suppliers of complementary goods. Purchases must be made before other buyers come on the scene. Purchases must be made according to complex time schedules and before profits can be made from associated operations. Circumstances and company goals set time limits for practically every kind of negotiation and for buyers and sellers alike. Negotiators should try to determine beforehand what the other side's time constraints are. Hopefully, theirs will be shorter than yours. But in any case negotiators can manipulate time limits, or at least the *perception* of time limits, to their advantage.

Japanese bargainers have a big advantage when it comes to manipulation of time limits—an American's internal clock apparently ticks much faster and much louder. Impatience is perhaps our greatest weakness in international negotiations. We're interested in quick action and immediate results. In contrast, the Japanese executive tends to take a more careful approach to business transactions. Long-term steady growth is valued over short-term fantastic results. It is much more difficult to rush a Japanese decision by imposing a time limit because (1) the consensus approach generally takes longer and (2) the Japanese would rather make no decision than a bad one. Alternatively, most Americans would rather risk a bad decision than let a potential opportunity slip by.

Fourteen years ago, Howard Van Zandt wrote that negotiations in Japan will take "six times longer" than in the United States.[1] Things have changed somewhat since then, but more time should still be allotted for negotiations in Japan. Particularly important will be home office understanding and support. A copy of Van Zandt's article given to key headquarters personnel may help in this regard. The point is that American negotiators must lengthen their own time limits by convincing headquarters to expect things to take longer in Japan.

Americans in Japan can also manipulate the Japanese side's perception of their time limits by making hotel reservations for longer or shorter periods than expected. Most foreign clients will check the length of your hotel reservations as part of their prenegotiation preparation. Your reservations will influence their behavior. Upon your arrival, you will also be asked how long you expect to stay in Japan. Negotiators should be aware that something simple like a hotel reservation communicates much, and this channel of communication should be used to your advantage, not theirs.

Another factor related to the timing of negotiations is Japanese holidays (see Table 5-1). Negotiations might be scheduled to use the holidays as a lever. Such tactics are often used by foreign business people against Americans—scheduling talks right before Christmas, for example.

Finally, in some circumstances it may be possible to impose time limits on Japanese negotiators by setting deadlines. For example, we

Table 5-1. Public Holidays in Japan.

January 1	New Year's Day
January 1-3	Bank Holidays (banks reopen on January 4)
January 15	Coming of Age Day
February 11	National Foundation Day
March 21	Vernal Equinox Day (date changes from year to year)
April 29	The Emperor's Birthday
May 1	May Day (most manufacturers closed, service firms open)
May 3	Constitution Memorial Day
May 5[a]	Children's Day[a]
September 15	Respect for the Aged Day
September 23	Autumn Equinox Day (date changes from year to year)
October 10	Physical Culture Day
November 3	Culture Day
November 23	Labor Thanksgiving Day
December 29	New Years Holiday begins (lasts about 5 to 10 days)

Note: Many businesses are beginning to observe a five-day week, but most blue-collar workers put in a half day on Saturdays. If a holiday falls on Sunday, it is observed the next day.

a. From April 29 to May 5 is "Golden Week." Some firms remain closed the entire time. Some manufacturers close for a week during the summer.

have heard of one American capital equipment supplier who told his Japanese clients that "beginning on Monday, for every day you delay your decision the price goes up $10,000." So on Monday the price was $100,000, Tuesday $110,000, and they bought on Wednesday at $120,000. Such a story is entertaining but we recommend avoiding such threats and deadlines. The only reason the American got the order is because the Japanese had no alternative *at that time.*

There is no doubt that the American's threats precluded a long-term relationship and any future orders. The imposition of time limits should only be used in extreme circumstances and accompanied with an explanation. Even a comment such as, "When can we expect to hear from you?," translates into Japanese as inappropriate impatience. It is probably best to say nothing at all. American bargainers should understand the Japanese decision process, anticipate that things will move more slowly, and plan accordingly.

NOTE TO CHAPTER 5

1.   Howard Van Zandt, "How to Negotiate in Japan," *Harvard Business Review* (Novermber–December 1970): 45–56.

6 AT THE NEGOTIATION TABLE

The most difficult aspect of an international business negotiation is the actual conduct of the face-to-face meeting. Assuming that the appropriate people have been chosen to represent your firm, and that those representatives are well prepared, and that the situational factors have been manipulated in your favor, things can still go wrong at the negotiation table. Obviously, if these other preliminaries haven't been managed properly, then things *will* go wrong during the meetings.

In Chapter 2 we mentioned four stages of business negotiations— (1) nontask sounding, (2) task-related information exchange, (3) persuasion, and (4) concessions and agreement. We pointed out that international business negotiations all over the world tend to follow this sequence of events. We also suggested that some of the major differences between the American and Japanese negotiation styles regard the importance of and time spent on each of the four steps. Our presentation of recommendations regarding the face-to-face meetings with Japanese clients is ordered according to these four stages typical in most business negotiations.

NONTASK SOUNDING

Americans always discuss topics other than business at the negotiation table. But we're quick about it. We move the discussion to the specific business at hand usually after five or ten minutes. There is a purpose, beyond friendliness and politeness, to this preliminary talk. Before getting to the business at hand it is important to learn how the other side feels *this particular day.*

We also learn how to communicate to our clients by learning about their backgrounds and interests. To the extent that people's backgrounds are similar, communication can be more efficient. Engineers can use technical jargon when talking to other engineers; golfers can use golfing analogies; family men and women can compare the cash drain of a fledgling business unit to putting kids through college.

During these initial stages of conversation we also make judgments about the people with whom we will be dealing. Can he be trusted? Will she be reliable? How much power does he have in his organization? Such assessments are made before business discussions even begin.

Perhaps this sounds like a lot to accomplish in five to ten minutes, but that's how long it usually takes in the United States. Not so in Japan. The goals of the nontask sounding are identical, but the time spent is far longer. In the United States we depend on our lawyers to get us out of bad deals if we've made a mistake in sizing up our clients or vendors. In Japan lawyers aren't used for such purposes. Instead, Japanese executives spend substantial time and effort in nontask sounding so that problems requiring lawyers don't develop later.

Nontask Sounding for Top Executives

The role of top executives in Japanese negotiations is ceremonial. Ordinarily they are brought into negotiations only to sign the agreement after all issues have been settled by lower level executives. On occasion, top executives are included earlier in the talks to communicate commitment and importance. In either case, their main activity is nontask sounding.

Getting top American executives to understand the importance of nontask sounding and make these adjustments in their behavior may be difficult. One successful way has been to supply them with a list of appropriate questions to ask during the *aisatsu* and other such meetings. (See Exhibit 6–1 for a hypothetical example of such a list.) The questions and topics can be assembled using information from

---

Exhibit 6-1. Hypothetical Agenda for Top Executive Non-task Sounding.

Date & Time: 11:00 a.m. August 25, 1983

Meeting With: Mr. Ichiro Matsuyama, Senior Councillor of the Mitsuichi Bank

Location: MITSUICHI Bank Headquarters
Otemachi, 1-Chome
Chiyoda-ku, Tokyo

Purpose of the Visit:
Courtesy call and to thank him for the kind introduction to the chairman and the president of ABC Corporation.

Suggested Topics:

— Thank him for sharing busy time with us.

— Talk about bamboo jogging board Mr. Suzuki, chairman of Mitsuichi Bank, California subsidiary, gave. Mr. Matsuyama also uses it.

— Report to him that a former ambassador to Japan and a mutual friend fully recovered from a recent illness to the point that he can play golf again.

— Report to him how the meeting proceeded at ABC Corporation Headquarters, and thank him for his junior executives' support. (Names of Junior executives: Mr. Suzuki and Mr. Ikeyama, California subsidiary, Messers. Kojima and Ohmori of Mitsuichi Bank, Kyoto Branch.)

— Ask him about his reaction to the recent acquisition of Bank of California by the Japanese bank.

— Ask when he is scheduled to visit Los Angeles again. Promise to play golf with him during his visit. Invite him to visit Los Angeles during the Olympics with a lot of Japanese yen to spend.

Background Information:
You met with Mr. Matsuyama last year when you were invited by MITI (Ministry of International Trade and Industry) and JETRO (Japan External Trade Organization). That meeting was arranged at the U.S. Ambassador's suggestion. The Ambassador was willing to provide a letter of introduction to Mr. Matsuyama.

Two days ago Mr. Matsuyama visited the chairman of ABC Corporation to introduce you and your profile.

the Japan "Who's Who" and a resume supplied by the Japanese company. Many Japanese firms have resumes on hand that contain key personal information of top executives for such purposes. The Japanese will also want the *aisatsu* and associated top-level meting to go smoothly. The conduct of such meetings is critical in Japan, and surprises at this stage are best avoided.

Another way to induce top American executives to behave properly is to emphasize that in Japanese conversation, what is said is not as important as how it is said. The Japanese top executive is making gut level judgments about the integrity, reliability, commitment, and humility (if the Japanese is considerably older or his company is more powerful) of his American counterpart. Moreover, from the American perspective, the content of the talk—the words and verbal information—may seem inane. But from the Japanese point of view the content of the talk—the nonverbal messages and feelings conveyed, the *wa*—will be critical.

A few other details regarding nontask sounding at top levels should be mentioned. First, business cards may or may not be exchanged. The American executives should be prepared with cards in Japanese and exchange them if the other side offers. However, when presidents of companies meet, business cards often are not required. In such cases, American presidents should be very familiar with their Japanese counterparts in advance. Second, small gifts are appropriate. Examples are pens, ties, or desktop ornaments, all with your company's logo. Anything that cuts (scissors, letter openers) and handkerchiefs should not be given, as such items symbolize the severing of relationships in Japan. The thought is what counts in this exchange of gifts, and very expensive gifts are unnecessary and actually inappropriate, even for presidents of Japanese firms. Third, a vague or implied reference to the future business relationship is appropriate toward the end of the *aisatsu*. It should be remembered, however, that indirectness and vagueness are key. Comments such as the following are appropriate:

1. "We would be glad to be of assistance to you in any way in the future."
2. "We pride ourselves in our high-quality products and we hope you share our views."
3. "Your company and our company appear to share some common goals."

Alternatively, comments as substantive as the following are inappropriate, even boorish, from the Japanese perspective.

1. "I hope you will consider our firm for your advertising services in the United States."
2. "A distribution agreement involving our two firms would prove profitable for both."
3. "If we can come to some agreement on the tough question of price, then the rest of the issues are minor."

Finally, when high level meetings are held in the United States, we recommend the Japanese approach. Top-level Japanese executives will not be prepared to bargain and will not be persuaded, even when in the United States. It's simply not their role. When American hosts wish to demonstrate the importance of the visit and the deal, we advise sending a limousine to pick up the Japanese party at their hotel. The initial meeting between top executives should not be held across a boardroom table, and certainly not across the American executive's desk. Rather, a more comfortable, living room atmosphere is preferable.

Nontask Sounding for Lower Level Executives

In the United States business relationships are typically established using the following procedures. First a letter of introduction, then a phone call for an appointment, then a meeting at the client's office (including five to ten minutes of nontask sounding followed by the business proposal), and perhaps lunch, with more business talk. Almost always, after five to ten minutes of nontask sounding, an American client will ask, "Well now, what can I do for you?"

In Japan the typical routine goes something like the following. The initial appointment will be set up and attended by the *shokai-sha*. The Japanese client will invite the American party, including the *shokai-sha*, for a late afternoon meeting at the Japanese firm's offices. There the Americans will meet the concerned operational level personnel for a chat that does not include business talk or proposals. The same topics appropriate for the *aisatsu* are appropriate here, but business is not to be discussed yet. At around 6:00 P.M. the Japanese will suggest dinner. Ordinarily, they will pick the restaurant and pick up the tab. Americans won't have a chance to fight for the bill because they will never see one. Business talk will still be inappropriate. After dinner the Japanese will suggest a few drinks at a Ginza night club. There, more nontask sounding, including sharing drinks and conversation with the bar hostesses, will be the bill of fare. These sessions will ordinarily go on past 11:00 P.M. and end with a scheduling of future meetings. Throughout this first afternoon and evening of introductions, only vague and indirect references to a future relationship may be made, but we advise they be mentioned only in response to similar comments by the Japanese. As in the *aisatsu*, the Japanese will be looking for integrity, sincerity, a cooperative attitude, and *wa*. Economics will come later.

Other minor considerations: Business cards will be required and small gifts (exchanged before leaving the offices) will be appropriate. For meetings in the United States, setting and formality will be marginally less important for operational level executives, but not much less. Particularly when the Japanese firm is the one courted, more of a Japanese approach—long periods of nontask sounding including dinner at a very good restaurant or at your home—is advised.

TASK-RELATED EXCHANGE OF INFORMATION

Only after the nontask sounding is complete and the *wa* is established should business be introduced. American executives are advised to let the Japanese signal when the task-related exchange of information should start. Typically, such signals will be given after tea or coffee has been served and may include a statement such as, "Can you tell me more about your company?" or "Tell me, what has brought you to Japan?"

A task-related exchange of information implies a two-way communication process. However, it has been the observation of several authors that when Americans meet Japanese across the negotiation table, the information flow is unidirectional—American to Japanese. In the paragraphs to follow we will recommend actions for American bargainers that will help them to manage efficiently the give and take of information.

Giving Information

The most obvious problem associated with providing information to Japanese clients will be the language. It is true that many more Japanese executives can speak and understand English than Americans can Japanese. English is, after all, the international language of business and technology. However, Americans should be careful of misunderstandings arising from the Japanese side's limited knowledge of English. Confusion can result when Japanese executives, because of politeness, indicate they understand when in fact they do not. When any doubt exists Americans should use visual media (slides, brochures) and provide copious written support materials and an interpreter if the Japanese side hasn't. Even when the Japanese side does provide an interpreter, there may be critical stages of the negotiations when your own interpreter should be included on your negotiation team.

In a 1970 article published in the *Harvard Business Review*, entitled "How to Negotiate in Japan," author Howard Van Zandt made several recommendations regarding the use of interpreters in business negotiations.[1] Fourteen years ago his advice was accurate. Now, however, higher quality interpreters are available and a few of his recommendations simply don't apply. Table 6–1 includes all of his recommendations and our dissenting comments. If interpreter problems do surface during your negotiations you should make a change. But be certain the replacement is a definite improvement. More than one interpreter change can cause serious disruptions of the negotiations. Finally, you should be aware that interpreters are available who specialize in business, engineering, or government, and an appropriate one should be selected for your negotiations.

Once you are comfortable with the language situation, you can turn your attention to more subtle aspects of giving information to the Japanese. The first of these has to do with the order of presentation. In the United States we tend to say what we want and explain the reasons behind our request only if necessary. That's why the task-related exchange of information goes so quickly. This isn't the Japanese way. Recall the description of the *naniwabushi* in Chapter 3 — long explanation followed by the request followed by expressions of sorrow for the request. Given this mode of operation, it is not surprising to hear the American executive's complaint about the thousands of questions the Japanese ask. The Japanese expect long explanations. Thus, Americans should be prepared with detailed information to back up their proposal. Appropriate technical experts should be included on negotiation teams; their contribution *will be* required. Finally, we recommend a Japanese style of presentation. Background and explanations should be presented first, and only

Table 6-1. Van Zandt's Recommendations Regarding Interpreters. (*Amended by Authors*).

---

1. Brief the interpreter in advance about the subject and give him a copy of the presentation to study and discuss.

2. Speak loudly, clearly, and slowly. (Some Americans try to talk with a cigar in the mouth—an egregious mistake.)

3. Avoid little-known words, such as "arcane," "heuristic," or "buncombe."

4. Maintain a pleasant attitude.

5. Explain each major idea in two or three different ways, as the point may be lost if discussed only once.

6. Do not talk more than a minute or two without giving the interpreter a chance to speak.

7. While talking, allow the interpreter time to make notes of what is being said.

8. Assume that all numbers over 10,000 may be mistranslated. Repeat them carefully and write them down for all to see. The Japanese system of counting large sums is so different from that of the West that errors frequently occur. Also, the number billion should be avoided, as it means 1,000,000,000,000 in Europe, and 1,000,000,000 in the United States.

(Amended)

9. Do not lose confidence if the interpreter uses a dictionary. No one is likely to have a vocabulary of 40,000 words in each of two languages, and a dictionary is often essential.	9. We disagree. Having to use a dictionary is a sign of potentially serious problems.

(Amended)

10. Permit the interpreter to spend as much time as needed in clarifying points whose meanings are obscure.	10. If the interpreter is spending more time than you in talking, then he is doing more than translating. This may help or hurt you.

11. Do not interrupt the interpreter as he translates. Interrupting causes many misunderstandings, usually leaves the visitor from overseas only half informed, and gives the Japanese side a feeling that the foreigner is too impatient to be competent.

12. Do not jump to conclusions, as Japanese ways of doing things are often different from what foreigners expect.

13. Avoid long sentences, double negatives, or the use of negative wordings of a sentence when a positive form could be used.

Table 6-1. continued

14. Don't use slang terms, as, for example, "If you will let me have half a 'G' at six bits a piece, it'll be gung ho with me." Rather, state simply, "I want 500 at 75¢ each."

15. Avoid superfluous words. Your point may be lost if wrapped up in generalities.

16. Try to be as expressive as possible by using movements of hands, eyes, lips, shoulders, and head to supplement words.

17. During meetings, write out the main points discussed; in this way both parties can double check their understanding.

18. After meetings, confirm in writing what has been agreed to.

19. Don't expect an interpreter to work for over an hour or two without a rest period. His work is exhausting and a nervous strain.

	(Amended)
20. Consider using two men if interpreting is to last a whole day or into the evening, so that when one tires the other can take over.	20. This is only true in cases of "simultaneous" translation, as opposed to the usual "consecutive" translation used in most business transactions.
	(Amended)
21. Don't be suspicious if a speaker talks for five minutes and the interpreter covers it in half a minute. The speaker may have been wordy.	21. Be suspicious. This can be a sign that the interpreter is fatigued or simply not paying attention.
	(Amended)
22. Be understanding if it develops that the interpreter has made a mistake. It is almost impossible to avoid making some errors, because Japanese and European languages are so dissimilar.	22. Mistakes are a sign of the interpreter's incompetence. Often in major negotiations, minor mistakes can result in break up of the negotiation.

23. Be sure the Japanese are given all the time they want to tell their side of the story. If they hesitate, ask the interpreter for advice on what next to say or do.

Source: Howard Van Zandt, "How to Negotiate in Japan," *Harvard Business Review* (November-December 1970): 45-56.

toward the end should the actual request or proposal be made. Such an approach will take longer, but it will obtain better results with Japanese clients.

It should be noted that we do not recommend the third step of *naniwabushi*, the *urei*. Such an expression of sorrow requires subtle nuances and special circumstances to be effective. *Urei* attempted by even the most informed and experienced American negotiators will appear completely out of context and, therefore, insincere. In any case, most American negotiators would view such behavior as going too far.

Another reason for the many questions the Japanese ask has to do with their consensus decisionmaking style. Several people on their side may ask for the same information or explanation. Most Americans find this repetitive questioning irritating and even insulting. "Didn't they believe me the first time?" But such tactics should be viewed in light of the Japanese decisionmaking process in which everyone must be convinced. You should also realize that interrogation may be a tactic to make sure your explanation holds up under close scrutiny. Therefore, we recommend patience and the kind of detailed preparations necessary to prevent inconsistent answers.

Clearly then, communicating your bargaining position, your company's needs and preferences, will take longer in Japan. Language problems and required explanations will require more meetings, involving more of your people (technical experts) and more of theirs. We strongly recommend patience with this process and the anticipation of increased time and money at this stage. But at some point American bargainers will have to terminate such questioning. While answering a thousand questions may be tedious but necessary, answering two thousand questions may not be productive. We suggest the following tactics for ending the Japanese side's questions:

1. Summarize your previous answer after such statements as the following: "I already gave that information to Suzuki-san yesterday, but to reiterate. . . ." or "That's the same question we talked about before, but I'll go over it again."
2. Offer to write down the requested information so that it may be shared with all concerned Japanese executives.
3. Generally, a repeated question should be answered the second time in about ten minutes. The third time it's asked the answer should be a one-minute summary. If the same question is asked a

fourth time, it's probably a persuasive tactic and not information gathering. The appropriate response is then silence or a change of subject.

We have heard of Japanese bargainers in Tokyo asking their New York office to verify price quotes with your New York office. In Japan, as well as in the United States, this is pushing the questioning too far. We suggest expression of your company's irritation through your informal communication channel or, if necessary, at the table using a more tactful approach such as, "Let's consolidate our channels of communication and not involve my New York office. I am representing my firm here and what New York has to say doesn't pertain."

Finally, we recommend that American bargainers guard against the tendency of making concessions during this exchange of information. We have found that often American negotiators, impatient with the process, will actually make concessions during this second stage of negotiations, before they have even determined the Japanese negotiator's position. It will take great patience indeed to avoid the natural urge to get to the third stage, persuasion, by making concessions in the hopes that the Japanese will reciprocate.

Getting Information

Hopefully, your Japanese clients will be courting your business. In such a situation they will be the ones making proposals and supplying you with more information than you probably want. But should your firm be initiating the contact or trying to make the sale, expect great difficulties getting feedback to your proposals. If you ask a group of Japanese executives what they think of your price quote and proposal, they will invariably say, "Oh, it looks fine." They will respond in such a manner even if they think it stinks.

Let's review the reasons behind this seemingly unfathomable behavior. The first regards consensus decisionmaking. No Japanese, especially the boss, feels qualified to speak for the group before a consensus has been reached. Second, the Japanese executive wishes to maintain the *wa*; from his point of view a negative, albeit honest, answer at the negotiation would disrupt the harmony established. Finally, American executives are unable to read the subtle, nonverbal, negative cues that accompany the "Oh, it looks fine." Another Japanese executive would read the nonverbal message that "it stinks," but even the most experienced Americans won't be able to process this implied message.

Just as Japanese executives speak a different language, their nonverbal behaviors also have different meanings. We have found in both simulated and real business negotiations that the Japanese conversational style includes much less eye contact than does the American one. When Americans bargain with the Japanese this difference seems to cause problems for both sides. Japanese report discomfort at the "aggressive staring" of the Americans. Americans suggest that something must be wrong because the Japanese "won't look me in the eye." Eye contact and eye movements, ordinarily a source of information about other's feelings, don't communicate across cultural barriers.

In the United States, another key source of information regarding your client's reaction to your proposals is his or her facial expression. Most of us process such information unconsciously, but we all do pay attention to this channel. Indeed, many American executives report great frustration because of the Japanese negotiator's "poker face." However, we have found by studying videotapes of simulated business negotiations that there appears to be little difference between Japanese and Americans in the quantity of facial expressions. The inscrutability of the former has more to do with the timing and cultural rules for facial expressions than with intentionally trying to keep negotiating partners in the dark. See Exhibit 6–2 for one author's explanation of such rules for facial expressions in Japan.

These are the reasons why in our interviews we have heard very experienced Americans report, "I make deals all over the world. And everywhere I go I can pretty much tell where I stand with my clients. Everywhere, that is, except Japan." So, how can Americans get at the *honne*, or true mind of the Japanese negotiators? The *tatemae* (official stance) of the negotiation table often isn't very helpful. The only way Americans can be privy to the *honne* is through an informal channel of communication. And this informal channel can only be established between and through the lowest levels of the negotiation teams. This is perhaps the primary reason for including lower level executives on your negotiation team. It will be almost impossible for one American to handle both the formal communication at the negotiation table and the informal communications after hours.

Exhibit 6-2. The Japanese Smile.

A Japanese can smile in the face of death, and usually does. . . . There is neither defiance nor hypocrisy in the smile; nor is it to be confounded with that smile of sickly resignation which we are apt to associate with weakness of character. It is an elaborate and long cultivated etiquette. It is also a silent language. But any effort to interpret it according to Western notions of physiognomical expression would [not be successful].

[The] first impression is, in most cases, wonderfully pleasant. The Japanese smile at first charms. It is only at a later day, when one has observed the same smile under extraordinary circumstances—in moments of pain, shame, disappointment—that one becomes suspicious of it. Its apparent inopportuneness may even, on certain occasions, cause violent anger. . . . The Japanese child is born with this happy tendency, which is fostered through all the period of home education. . . . The smile is taught like the bow; like the prostration; . . . But the smile is to be used upon all pleasant occasions, when speaking to a superior or to an equal, and even upon occasions which are not pleasant; it is part of deportment. The most agreeable face is the smiling face; and to present always the most agreeable face possible to parents, relatives, teachers, friends, well-wishers, is a rule of life. . . . Even though the heart is breaking, it is a social duty to smile bravely."

Source: Lafcadio Hearn, *Glimpses of Unfamiliar Japan* (Boston: Houghton Mifflin, 1894), p. 656-683.

Management of this informal channel of communication will be critical for efficient and successful negotiations, and therefore an important yet delicate undertaking. Your lowest level bargainer should be assigned the task of establishing a relationship of trust with an operational level manager on the Japanese side during the nontask sounding activities. The *shinyo* is critical. During the task-related exchange of information, indeed throughout the negotiations, time should be spent after hours nurturing this relationship. Such a relationship can be initiated by simply asking the selected Japanese executive out for a drink, "to solve our companies' problems." The Japanese side will also be looking to open such a channel of communication, and the American side should be alert for such overtures.

At first, all this may appear a bit sneaky and even unethical to the American reader. It seems the opposite of laying your cards on the table. But it makes perfect sense from the Japanese perspective.

The *honne* can be communicated without risk through a low-level executive, who makes no commitments as he or she speaks and who saves the face of the American managers and preserves the *wa* between the higher level negotiators. This may seem a monumental waste of time to an American, but we have learned through experience that negotiations with Japanese proceed smoothly when this informal channel of communication is managed properly.

Once this informal channel of communication has been opened, it will be used for aggressive persuasive tactics and for assessing how each side really feels about the involved proposals and the arguments. Such information will be communicated after hours over drinks, in restaurants, night clubs, and at bath houses. It will emanate from and be transmitted to all members of the negotiation team. But despite the fact that everyone knows about this "under the table" channel of communication, it is critical that it remain just that. Any reference to such a channel (e.g., "Suzuki-san told Mr. Smith last night that . . .") will lead to immediate dismissal of Suzuki-san from the negotiations and, thus, elimination of the "leak."

As an example of how important this informal channel can be we tell the following story. One large American firm that we have worked with sought to acquire a smaller Japanese firm. Talks between executives of the two companies had not been fruitful. Although the Japanese executives showed initial interest in the deal, and the American firm had a final proposal ready, the Japanese seemed hesitant. The American side decided on a wait-and-see strategy and nothing happened for almost six months. Then a lower level manager of the American firm received a call from an acquaintance in the Japanese firm, asking for an appointment. Over a drink the Japanese explained why there were delays: "I have something to tell you that just couldn't be talked about by my boss to your boss. . . ." And he went on to explain the primary problems from the Japanese point of view—the acquisition price and the renaming of the company. Once out in the "open," the companies were able to deal with both issues. But the Japanese side simply felt it inappropriate to use a formal communication channel at the negotiation table to voice such objections to a higher status buyer and potential owner.

One final point should be made about the task-related exchange of information. Often, one negotiation team member will be assigned notetaking responsibilities only. Another common practice is to tape record meetings, ordinarily with the other side's permission. The intent is to have the tapes available for careful review later. Americans may also wish to tape the meetings. At the very least notes should be taken during the meeting. We have found it useful to keep a tally of the topics of Japanese questions. That is, if the Japanese ask about delivery schedules six times and service contracts only twice, then they are signaling the importance of delivery.

In the event that an informal channel of communication cannot be established between lower level members of each firm's negotiation team, then the *shokai-sha* or *chukai-sha* can be used in such a way. Perhaps they will be able to set up the necessary relationship by inviting the two appropriate lower level executives out for dinner. However, this option should be exercised only as a last resort because of the added communication problems associated with a less involved third party and because it is best to keep *shokai-sha* and *chukai-sha* in reserve. That is, if *shokai-sha* and *chukai-sha* fail, then the business is over.

PERSUASION

We hope that it is evident from the above discussion that in Japan there is not a clear separation of the task-related exchange of information and persuasion. The two stages tend to blend together as each side more clearly defines and refines its needs and preferences. So much time is spent at this task-related exchange of information that little is left to "argue" about during the persuasion stage. Indeed, Robert March reports that Japanese negotiators tend to prepare for negotiations in a way very different from Americans:

> They developed defensive arguments with no consideration of persuading or selling or converting the other side. Nor did they consider what the other side might be thinking or offering, nor of anticipated strategies, nor of any concession strategies.
>
> A strong consensus was reached based on the arguments supporting their position after the leader had reviewed these and everyone had noted them down. There was strong group cohesion.[2]

However, from the American perspective persuasion is the heart of a negotiation. In America we have a wide range of persuasive tactics that can be and often are employed to change our clients' minds. Researchers at the Kellogg School of Business Administration at North-

Table 6-2. Bargaining Tactics.

Positive Influence Tactics

Promise. A statement in which the source indicates his or her intention to provide the target with a reinforcing consequence which the source anticipates the target will evaluate as pleasant, positive or rewarding.

"If you can deliver the equipment by June 1st, we will make another order right away."

Recommendation. A statement in which the source predicts that a pleasant environmental consequence will occur to the target. Its occurrence is not under the source's control.

"If you keep the company name after the acquisition, then your present customers will stay with the company."

Reward. A statement by the source that is thought to create pleasant consequences for the target.

"This negotiation is progressing smoothly because you have prepared well."

Positive normative appeal. A statement in which the source indicates that the target's past, present, or future behavior was or will be in conformity with social norms.

"Lowering your price in light of the new information will demonstrate your interest in good principles of business."

Aggressive Influence Tactics

Threat. Same as promise, except that the reinforcing consequences are thought to be noxious, unpleasant, or punishing.

"If you insist on those terms we will have to find another suitor for our company."

Warning. Same as recommendation, except that the consequences are thought to be unpleasant.

"If we can't get together at this stage, few other companies will be interested in your proposal."

Punishment. Same as reward, except that the consequences are thought to be unpleasant.

"You can't possibly mean that. Only a fool would ask for such a high price."

Negative normative appeal. Same as positive normative appeal, except that the target's behavior is in violation of social norms.

"No one else we deal with requires that kind of guarantee."

Table 6-2. continued

Command. A statement in which the source suggests that the target perform a certain behavior.

"It's your turn to make a counteroffer."

Information Exchange Tactics

Commitment. A statement by the source to the effect that his future bids will not go below or above a certain level.

"We will deliver the equipment within three months, and at the price we originally quoted."

Self-Disclosure. A statement in which the source reveals information about itself.

"My company now requires an ROI of at least 15 percent during the first year."

Question. A statement in which the source asks the target to reveal information about itself.

"Why are you asking for such a high royalty payment?"

Source: Adapted from R. Angelmar and L.W. Stern, "Development of a Content Analytic System for Analysis of Bargaining Communication in Marketing," *Journal of Marketing Research* (February 1978): 93-102.

western University have come up with a list of such persuasive tactics. (See Table 6-2).

We have observed Americans using all such persuasive tactics. Perhaps the most interesting example of differing reactions of Japanese and Americans is in the use of "veiled" threats. We know of one American firm putting a "dog" business unit up for sale. They solicited bids from several American buyers whom they thought might be interested. However, only one takeover proposal was received. When the managers from the one interested company called on the executive in charge of the sale, they met in the executive's office. When substantive discussions began, that executive was careful to search through what appeared to be a stack of competitive proposals on his desk for the pertinent proposal. Thus, a subtle bluff or threat was made—"If you don't make some concessions, we'll talk to someone else." Those imaginary competitive proposals were never discussed, but the buyer did make concessions.

Be aware that the use of some of these tactics with Japanese clients would signal the end of bargaining. During a similar acquisition negotiation one of our Japanese clients called on an executive vice-president of the American selling firm. The American "happened" to have a letter from another possible buyer (the colorful logo on the letterhead was easily recognizable) on his desk. Another veiled threat, a bluff, or an accident? We don't know. Neither the letter nor other buyers were discussed. We do know, however, that the Japanese interpreted the letter on the desk as a threat and thereafter refused to consider dealing with that American company. Even a veiled threat is too strong a tactic to use with Japanese buyers.

Another important factor in Japan is the context in which specific tactics are used. Table 6–3 presents a list of persuasive tactics appropriate in Japan. At the negotiation table bargainers are limited to the use of questions, self-disclosures, and other positive influence behaviors. Aggressive influence tactics, which can only be used by negotiators in higher power positions, should be communicated through the low-level, informal communication channel. And even then, only subtle and indirect threats, commands, and so on, are appropriate. So this informal channel of communication is doubly important from the American perspective. First, it provides a method of more accurately reading Japanese clients, and, second, it makes available to American bargainers persuasive tactics that would be completely inappropriate during the formal talks.

To sum up, if an impasse is reached with Japanese clients, rather than trying to persuade in the usual American manner, we recom-

Table 6–3. Persuasive Tactics Appropriate for Negotiations with the Japanese.

At the Negotiation Table

1. Questions
2. Self-disclosures
3. Positive influence tactics
4. Silence
5. Change of subject
6. Recesses and delays
7. Concessions and commitments

Informal Channels and Buyers Only

1. Aggressive influence tactics

mend use of the following nine persuasive tactics, in the following order and in the following circumstances:

1. Ask more questions. We feel that the single most important advice we can give is to use questions as a persuasive tactic. This is true in not only Japan, but anywhere in the world including the United States. In his book, *Negotiation Game*, Chester Karrass suggests that sometimes it's "smart to be a little bit dumb" in business negotiations.[3] Ask the same questions more than once—"I didn't completely understand what you meant. Can you please explain that again." If your clients or potential business partners have good answers, then it's perhaps best if you compromise on the issue. But often, under close scrutiny, their answers aren't very good. And with such a weak position exposed they will be obligated to concede. Therefore questions can elicit key information and can be powerful persuasive devices.

2. Reexplain your company's situation, needs, and preferences.

3. Use other positive influence tactics.

4. If you are still not satisfied with their response, try silence. Let them think about it and give them an opportunity to change their position. However, you should recognize that the Japanese are the world's experts at the use of silence. If silence is a tactic you find difficult to use, you should at least be aware that your Japanese clients will use it frequently.

5. If tactics 1 through 4 produce no concessions it will be time to change the subject or call a recess and put to work the informal communication channel. But rather than going directly to the more aggressive tactics we recommend repeating the first four tactics. The questions and explanations may expose new information or objections that couldn't be broached at the negotiation table.

6. Aggressive influence tactics may be used in negotiations with Japanese only at great risk and in special circumstances. First, they should only be used via the informal channel, and even then they should be used in the most indirect manner possible. Rather than saying, "If your company can't lower its price, then we'll go to another supplier," it would be better to say, "Lower prices on the part of your company would go a long way toward our not having to consider other options available to us." Second, they should be used only when the American company is clearly in the stronger position. Even in these two circumstances, use of such aggressive

persuasive tactics will damage the *wa*, which may in the long run be to your company's disadvantage. If power relations ever shift, the Japanese will be quick to exploit the change in events. However, if the American side exercises restraint and maintains the *wa*, then if and when power relations shift, the Japanese side will consider the American company's interests.

This latter point is difficult for most Americans to believe. But we have witnessed Japanese executives behave in this way several times. For example, in the early 1970s International Multi-Food Company (IMFC) sold franchise rights for a Mr. Donut chain to Duskin, Ltd. in Japan. Initially, IMFC provided the know-how (operations and marketing) for a successful venture in Japan. Since then, Duskin has turned Mr. Donut into the largest doughnut chain in Japan. Indeed, the franchise revenues from Duskin now exceed the total profits IMFC makes from its U.S. operations. When IMFC executives recently met with Duskin to renegotiate the franchise agreement, they anticipated substantial changes in the agreement to reflect the change in power relations. An American franchisee would certainly demand such an adjustment. However, because IMFC had been careful to maintain *wa* with the Japanese clients initially, the president of Duskin suggested only minor revisions to the agreement.

7. If tactics 1 through 6 have not produced Japanese concessions, we suggest the use of time to enable them to consider new information and to reach a consensus. The Japanese rarely make concessions immediately following persuasive appeals because everyone involved in the decision must be consulted and agree. Unfortunately, time is perhaps the most difficult tactic for American bargainers to use. We're in a hurry to solve the problem and settle the deal. "Letting things hang" goes against our nature. But it may be necessary. And hopefully they will run into their time limits before you run into yours. Also, use of this tactic will require the cooperation and understanding of your home office.

It should be remembered that the Japanese are skilled in the use of time as a persuasive tactic. Consensus decisionmaking and the long-term approach to business deals seems to enhance the effectiveness of tactical delays for Japanese bargaining with Americans.

8. The next persuasive tactic to use is asking the *chukai-sha* or *shokai-sha* to arbitrate your differences. Let them call your clients and meet as a go-between. We have seen *chukai-sha* successfully settle otherwise irreconcilable differences. For example, a major West

Coast retailer contacted Ernst & Whinney for *shokai-sha* services. They wished to be introduced to a Japanese sushi-bar chain that would participate in a "Japan Fair" promotion they had planned for several of their southern California stores. The *shokai-sha* introduced the vice-president of the retail chain to the appropriate executives of one of Japan's largest sushi chains and negotiations began. However, the Japanese seemed hesitant despite the several advantages of participation offered by the American company. They considered the expense of sending operational managers to the United States not worth the benefits of participation. So the somewhat exasperated American executives requested *chukai-sha* services. The *chukai-sha* acted as a mediator and presented again the benefits of the proposal—promotion and market research in the United States and use of the trip to Los Angeles as a reward for employees. Through the persuasive efforts of *chukai-sha* the deal was finally struck. However, serious consideration should be given to making concessions yourself before calling in *chukai-sha*. Third-party arbitration will ordinarily work only once.

9. Finally, if all else fails, it may be necessary to bring together the top executives of the two companies in the hope of stimulating more cooperation. However, such a tactic may fail, particularly if negative influence tactics have been used in the past. A refusal at this stage means the business is finished.

To conclude our discussion of persuasive tactics, we want to emphasize the importance of our recommendations. A mistake at this stage, even a minor one, can have major consequences for your Japanese business. American managers will have to be doubly conscientious to avoid blunders here because the Japanese style of persuasion is so different and apparently cumbersome. Remember that the Japanese are looking to establish a long-term business relationship of mutual benefit. Threats and the like don't fit into their understanding of how such a relationship should work. You should also recognize that we are recommending adoption of a Japanese approach to persuasion when bargaining with Japanese clients and business partners. We realize it takes longer, but in the end you and your company will benefit by such an approach. Finally, smart American negotiators will anticipate the Japanese use of the nine persuasive tactics just described.

CONCESSIONS AND AGREEMENT

The final stage of business negotiations involves concessions, building toward agreement. Negotiation requires compromise. Usually, both sides give up something to get even more. But the approach used for compromise differs on each side of the Pacific.

American managers report great difficulties in measuring progress. After all, in America you're half done when half the issues are settled. But in Japan nothing seems to get settled. Then, surprise, you're done. Often, Americans make unnecessary concessions right before agreements are announced by the Japanese. For example, we know of an American retail goods buyer traveling to Japan to buy six different consumer products for a large chain of discount department stores on the West Coast. He told us that negotiations for his first purchase took an entire week. In the United States, such a purchase would be consummated in an afternoon. So by his calculations, he expected to have to spend six weeks in Japan to complete his purchases. He considered raising his purchase prices to try to move things along faster. But before he was able to make such a concession, the Japanese quickly agreed on the other five products in just three days. This particular businessman was, by his own admission, lucky in his first encounter with Japanese bargainers.

This American businessman's near blunder reflects more than just a difference in decisionmaking style. To the American, a business negotiation is a problem-solving activity, the best deal for both parties being the solution. To a Japanese businessman, a business negotiation is a time to develop a business relationship with the goal of long-term mutual benefit. The economic issues are the *context*, not the *content*, of the talks. Thus, settling any one issue really isn't important. Such details will take care of themselves once a viable, harmonious business relationship is established. And, as happened in the case of our retail goods buyer, once the relationship was established—signaled by the first agreement—the other "details" were settled quickly.

American bargainers in Japan should expect this holistic approach and be prepared to discuss all issues simultaneously and in an apparently haphazard order. Progress in the talks should not be measured by how many issues have been settled. Rather, Americans must try to gauge the quality of the business relationship. Important signals of progress will be:

1. Higher level Japanese executives being included in the discussions;
2. Their questions beginning to focus on specific areas of the deal;
3. A softening of their attitudes and position on some of the issues— "Let us take some time to study this issue"; and
4. Increased bargaining and use of the lower level, informal channel of communication.

In Chapter 5 we discussed the importance of a documented concession strategy prepared before negotiations begin. Americans need to follow such strategies with care. Trading concessions with Japanese bargainers will not work because they view nothing to be settled until everything is settled. We advise making no concession until all issues and interests have been exposed and fully discussed. Then concessions should be made, on minor issues first, to help establish the relationship.

Concessions should not be decided upon at the negotiation table. Rather, Americans are advised to reconsider each concession away from the social pressure of the formal negotiations. This again is a Japanese practice. Because of the nature of the consensus decision-making, you will find the Japanese having to "check with the home office." It is a negotiation practice that Americans will do well emulating, particularly in Japan. Having limited authority can be an important check on concession making.

MINOR DISTRACTIONS

Before closing our discussion of the process of business negotiations it is important to mention briefly three Japanese behaviors that will seem rude to American bargainers but are nothing more than common habits for Japanese executives. First, the Japanese will often break into side conversations, in Japanese. Ordinarily, the purpose of this side conversation is clarification of something Americans have said. Second, often Japanese executives will enter or leave negotiations in the middle of your comments. This reflects their busy schedule and a different view of "meeting etiquette." Finally, it can be particularly disturbing to be talking to a group of Japanese and discover that one, perhaps even the senior executive, is "listening with his eyes shut." (This is the Japanese description for sleeping during meetings.) Again, this shouldn't be taken personally; it simply reflects a different view of appropriate behavior at meetings.

NOTES TO CHAPTER 6

1. Howard Van Zandt, "How to Negotiate in Japan," *Harvard Business Review* (November–December 1970): 45–56.
2. Robert M. March, "Business Negotiation as Cross-Cultural Communication: The Japanese–Western Case," *Cross Currents* 9, no. 1 (Spring 1982): 55–65.
3. Chester A. Karrass, *The Negotiating Game* (New York: Crowell, 1970).

7 AFTER NEGOTIATIONS

Once verbal agreements have been reached it is time to consider what follows the negotiations. In the United States executives talk of "concluding business deals." In Japan executives speak of "establishing business relationships." We've already discussed how such differing views influence negotiation processes. Now we will turn to the subject of how they influence postnegotiation procedures.

CONTRACTS

Contracts between American firms are often longer than 100 pages and include carefully worded clauses regarding every aspect of the agreement. American lawyers go to great lengths to protect their companies against all circumstances, contingencies, and actions of the other party (Exhibit 7-1). In this particular contract conditional phrases such as, "If . . . ," "In the event . . . ," and "Should . . . ," were used more than fifty times. The best contracts are the ones so tightly written that the other party would not think of going to court to challenge any provision. Our adversarial system requires such contracts.

In Japan, as in most other countries, legal systems are not depended upon to resolve disputes. Indeed, the term "disputes" doesn't reflect how a business relationship should work. Each side should be

---

Exhibit 7-1. Excerpt of an American Style Contract.

14.1 Should any circumstances preventing the complete or partial fulfillment by either of the parties of the obligations taken under this contract arise, namely: fire, floods, earthquake, typhoon, epidemics and other actions or force of nature, as well as war, military operations of any character, prohibitions of export or import, the time stipulated for the fulfillment of the obligations shall be extended for a period equal to that during which such circumstances will remain in force.

14.2 If these circumstances continue for more than six months, each of the parties shall have the right to refuse in full or in part from any further execution of the obligations under this contract and in such case neither of the parties shall have the right for reimbursement of any possible damages by the other party.

14.3 The party for whom it becomes impossible to meet its obligations under this contract shall immediately advise the other party as regards the commencement and cessation of the circumstances preventing the fulfillment of its obligations.

14.4 The delayed advice of the commencement or cessation of *force majeure* circumstances exceeding 15 days will deprive the party of the right to refer to these circumstances at a later date.

---

concerned about the mutual benefits of the relationship, and therefore consider the interests of the other. Consequently, in Japan written contracts are very short—two to three pages—are purposefully loosely written, and primarily contain comments on principles of the relationship (Exhibit 7–2). From the Japanese point of view, the American emphasis on tight contracts is tantamount to planning the divorce before the marriage. Klaus Schmidt puts it well:

> The Japanese feel that agreements require seasoning and maturity; as people work together, understandings become clearer and increasingly advantageous to both partners. As relationships and conditions change, the assumption is that performance expectations ought to change. Flexibility, adjustment, and pragmatics, then, dominate the execution of long-term contracts.[1]

Thus, contracts in Japan do not fulfill the same purposes as they do in the United States.

So what form should a contract between a Japanese and American firm take? There is no simple answer. It may have to be negotiated.

Exhibit 7-2. A Sample Japanese Style Contract.

Article 1:   This agreement is made this 4th day of October 1977 between "A" located in Tokyo, and "B" located in Shibuya-ku Tokyo, to maintain mutual prosperity and coexistence and lasting amicable relations.

Article 2:   B shall continuously develop products based upon all of B's copyrighted materials or designs, and actively conduct sales of such products in Japan and other nations. A shall not, without B's consent, have third parties in the aforementioned areas develop products based upon any of A's copyrighted materials or designs, provided, however, that this limitation shall not apply to written materials.

Article 3:   B may register designs to protect B's rights against third parties.

Article 4:   The content and proofreading of the said copyrighted materials shall be the responsibility of A.

Article 5:   The costs required for the writing of the said copyrighted materials shall be borne by A, and the costs of producing, selling and advertising shall be borne by B.

Article 6:   As a royalty for the production of A's copyrighted materials and designs, B shall pay A 3 percent of the cost thereof.

Article 7:   With A's consent, B shall have the right to have third parties produce totally or partially products based upon A's copyrighted materials or designs. In such cases, B shall pay A the royalty set forth in Article 6.

Article 8:   In the event that either A or B suffers damages due to violation by the other party of the terms set forth in this contract, the first party may claim damages.

Article 9:   Two identical counterparts are to be prepared, signed and sealed to evidence this contract, whereupon each party shall retain one copy.

A: _____

B: _____

Source: Graham and James attorneys.

It depends somewhat on the size and importance of the agreement and the size and experiences of the firms involved. Generally, larger deals justify the extra expense of including legal review by both Japanese and American lawyers. Large Japanese firms with histories of American contracts will understand the American's need for detailed contracts. Some Japanese, recognizing the increasing frequency of litigation between U.S. and Japanese firms, will specify the American approach. It is the executives of smaller Japanese firms, inexperienced in the ways of Americans, that may become suspicious when faced with lengthy fully detailed contracts. In these cases, it will be particularly important to explain the necessity of the legal review and detailed contract. However, you should realize that even with the most complete explanation not all Japanese executives will understand.

An American style contract will also cause considerable delays in signing. Japanese lawyers will tediously consider every detail. One rule of thumb suggests that every clause takes an entire day. Thus, something your legal counsel ordinarily reviews in three days will take at least three weeks in Tokyo.

It is difficult for us to make general recommendations regarding contracts. Many American executives of even the largest firms have been satisfied with a "compromise" contract when strong, long-standing personal relationships are involved. But each case is different. It is important that you and your firm push for the kind of contract you feel is necessary. Also, your legal counsel should be consulted on this issue.

SIGNING CEREMONIES

Informality being a way of life in the United States, even the largest contracts between American firms are often sent through the mail for signature. Here, ceremony is considered a waste of time and money. But when a major agreement is reached with a Japanese client or partner, the Japanese will expect the top executives involved to meet and sign the contract with ceremony. We recommend American firms accommodate these expectations. Below, a contract-signing ceremony is described involving Peter Magowan, the CEO of Safeway Stores, and Yotaro Kuroyanagi, the president of Allied Importing Company (AIC) of Japan. It represents the kind of ceremony that the Japanese expect and appreciate.

The presidents of each of the four retailers that make up the AIC consortium and the president of the joint venture flew to San Francisco for the signing ceremony. They and their staffs arrived at Safeway headquarters in Oakland at 3:00 P.M. (chauffeured from San Francisco) and were escorted to a large meeting room on the executive floor. Once everyone had arrived, Peter Magowan made a brief speech welcoming all and expressing pleasure at the agreement. Yotaro Kuroyanagi also made a speech echoing Magowan's remarks and thanking the hard-working negotiators on both sides. The four company presidents also came prepared to deliver similar remarks, but the staffs negotiated the agenda to preclude this sort of ceremony, which surely would have been necessary in Japan.

After the greetings by Magowan and Kuroyanagi, all six executives seated themselves, according to a prearranged ranking, for the actual signing. Gold Cross pens with the Safeway logo were supplied by the Safeway staff for the signing and to serve as gifts for the Japanese executives. During the signing pictures were taken by a professional photographer and two members of the Japanese staff.

Following the signing, gifts were exchanged. The Safeway staff produced decorative pieces of redwood, explaining that the gifts symbolized California and long-term business relations (California redwood is noted for its durability)—a thoughtful choice. One minor problem did occur. After the gift giving, the Japanese insisted on toasting the deal with champagne. So Safeway staff members arranged for Christian Brothers champagne and glasses. This was the first time alcoholic beverages had been consumed in the corporate offices at Safeway.

The signing ceremony was concluded after the champagne. All in all the ceremony took approximately forty-five minutes. In Japan such a ceremony would have been followed by an elaborate reception at the local Hotel Okura involving top executives and their staffs as well as others concerned—suppliers, advertising agency personnel, bankers, and so on.

HEADQUARTERS' ASSESSMENT
OF THE AGREEMENT

Often U.S. negotiators return to company headquarters with an agreement only to receive a mixed greeting. One executive told us, "The second half of the negotiation begins once I return to the home office." Headquarters, unaware of the requirements of business negotiations in Japan, will ask, "What took so long?" Ordinarily, all compromises and concessions have to be explained and justified in detail. Moreover, commitments requiring specific management actions must be delegated and ordered. All this can slow implementation and performance of the contract. In the worst cases, when negotiator and home office communications have been poor, negotiators have been required to renege and start over. When this occurs, the Japanese client or partner will either bypass this executive, who has lost face, and talk to those considered the real decisionmakers or decline further discussion, thus ending the relationship.

In Japan, as you might expect, everyone is pleased with negotiation outcomes. No one is blamed for shortcomings in the deal because all concerned managers participated in the negotiating and in the final decisionmaking. Even when profit goals haven't been met, Japanese executives are quick to emphasize their primary goal— establishing a harmonious, trusting business relationship. Moreover, because of the group decisionmaking and participation, all the action provisions of the agreement are quickly implemented.

It has been the experience of American firms that once the first deal has been struck with a Japanese client or partner all successive negotiations proceed quickly. Therefore, it is generally not necessary to send a complete negotiation team when new issues are to be considered. Clearly, then, it is best to start with a small, relatively simple business proposal. Once the relationship has been established, substantial and complex negotiations will proceed more smoothly. This is the approach used by Japanese firms entering the United States, and it is a sensible strategy when American firms court Japanese business.

FOLLOW-UP COMMUNICATIONS

Just as personal considerations are more important during negotiations with Japanese clients, they are also important after the negotiations are concluded. Obviously, you will be in touch with your Japanese clients and partners regarding the business of the relationship. But it will be equally important to keep personal relationships warm.

A formal letter should be sent from your top executive to their top executive expressing happiness that the talks have been concluded successfully and confidence that the new relationship will be prosperous and long lasting. But just as important as this formal correspondence will be short, more personal notes for each Japanese participant. It is a Japanese practice to include pictures of everyone to commemorate events and places associated with the negotiations— golf courses, Geisha houses, factory visits, and so on. This provides the much needed personal touch. The significance of these several follow-up notes is underscored by the recollection that all Japanese, top to bottom, were involved in the decisionmaking.

Another standard Japanese practice will be frequent visits to your headquarters. Negotiators traveling to the United States for other purposes will take the time to stop off and visit. Even if their primary purpose for the trip is a new account in New York, they will come to see you in Omaha. Again, such visits serve to keep the relationship warm and are a form of nontask sounding. Where Americans are urged by AT&T to "keep in touch" via telephone, Japanese will not use such a medium for such a purpose. The telephone and telex in Japan are used for business only. Therefore, personal comments should be reserved for face-to-face visits or letters. For example, we often send personal notes to our Japanese business associates that include published accounts of political and economic issues in which they might be interested.

One final consideration is crucial when doing business with the Japanese. Do not switch executives managing your Japanese business relationships. In dealing with American clients this is not much of a problem. Here the economics of the business deal are more important than the personal relationships involved. Managers often shift positions within companies and between companies. But in Japan most executives stay with the same company permanently. Moreover, Japanese executives are given long-term (five to ten years) responsibility for managing intercompany relationships. After all, much was invested in building the personal relations that make business between the companies work smoothly. So when American companies switch key managers, Japanese clients get very nervous. Therefore, such shifts should be made with great care, and should be accompanied by new efforts of nontask sounding and rapport building.

MODIFICATIONS TO AGREEMENTS

During the course of almost all business relationships changes occur in the environment and to either partner. For example, we know of a major Japanese trading company that agreed to purchase 6 million bushels of wheat at $1 per bushel. However, during the course of the contract the yen fell sharply in value relative to the dollar. The trading company had not budgeted for such a precipitous fluctuation in currency and was forced to renege. In such a situation in the United States the conflicts arising from the changing circumstance would be settled through the use of direct and confrontational legal channels or, as is now more often the case, in arbitration.

In Japan, given the same set of changing circumstances, companies would ordinarily resolve the conflicts through conferral. Thus, Japanese contracts often include such wording as, "All items not found in this contract will be deliberated and decided upon in a spirit of honesty and trust." When differences can't be ironed out through simple conferral, then the next step is to express concerns through *shokai-sha* or *chukai-sha* who hopefully can mediate a new understanding. Rarely will the confrontational and legal approaches be used in Japan, for they would destroy the harmony and trust required for continued business dealings. Even arbitration is viewed negatively in Japan. The Japanese Commercial Arbitration Association (JCAA) is designed both to educate executives on the option of arbitration and to conduct hearings in disputes. However, the process of arbitration is different in Japan. While in the United States the approach is usually one of confrontation, in Japan the overriding theme is compromise. The JCAA acts more like a *chukai-sha*, mediating and inducing settlements. Less than 1 percent of all cases brought to the JCAA end in binding arbitration.

Our recommendations are to include an international arbitration clause in your contract should conflicts arise. But even though such measures are included in the contract we suggest a Japanese approach to conflict resolution. That is, approach the dispute from a cooperative standpoint and talk with your Japanese client or partner. Given that you have maintained the *wa* and trust, and that you have an honest mutual interest in the deal, then such problems can usually be resolved through simple conferral. The next option is *chukai-sha* mediation. The last resort should be binding arbitration.

NOTE TO CHAPTER 7

1. Klaus D. Schmidt, *Doing Business in Japan* (Palo Alto, Cal.: Stanford Reford Research Institute International, 1978), pp. 21–22.

8 CULTURE AND PERSONALITY ISSUES

Some might suggest that the material we have presented in this book is the worst kind of stereotyping. Does everybody really act the same in Japan? Should we prejudge others based on their nationality or ethnic background? These are difficult but important questions, and we will attempt to answer them.

THE DANGERS OF STEREOTYPING

There is danger in stereotyping American executives. The same caveat must be made about Japanese bargainers. Indeed, any Japanese businessman would be quick to point out that personalities have a strong influence on bargaining styles. We certainly agree. In all dealings with Japanese clients you should consider the personalities of the bargainers involved.

Consider, for example, Akio Morita, founder and chairman of Sony Corporation—an unusual, albeit very successful, Japanese businessman. He has been described as outgoing, adventurous, and molded in the American entrepreneurial spirit. His top-down decisionmaking style is also well known. Such characteristics made him an outcast in Japanese industry initially, and his company concentrated on developing markets in the United States first. Soichiro Honda (founder and former chairman of Honda Motors) and Isao Nakauchi (chairman of Daiei, Japan's largest retailer) are also known

---

Exhibit 8-1.   Maverick Marketer—Japanese Chain Grows Fast, Helped by Alien Ways.

OSAKA—When Daiei Inc., a supermarket chain, wanted to get into the department store business a while ago, it adopted a strategy that would hardly surprise American executives: Daiei (pronounced die-ay) purchased about 10 percent of the stock of a major department store chain, Takashimaya, to obtain Takashimaya's help in opening department stores of its own.

For all the eyebrows raised in Japan's business circles, Daiei might as well have robbed a Shogun's grave. Buying a company's stock without its permission just isn't done here. Eventually, it took mediation by one of the country's biggest commercial banks to patch up the bad feelings between Takashimaya and Daiei. Even then, tongues wagged. Daiei was "unfamiliar with Japanese business practice," sniffed the *Yomiuri*, a major newspaper.

The incident wasn't the first time that Daiei had run afoul of Japan's business establishment, and, typically, Daiei's founder and president Isao Nakauchi, wasn't fazed. "Our way of thinking might be a step or two ahead of the era," says Mr. Nakauchi, who is generally respected by the Japanese executives but not celebrated for his modesty. "As time goes by (the others') way of thinking will change," he says.

A knack for ruffling feathers isn't the only un-Japanese trait of the company and its founder. Daiei shows little of the typical Japanese company's preference for decisions by consensus and none of the traditional disdain for growth through acquisitions. Many Japanese companies export heavily: Daiei imports heavily. And unlike the typical big Japanese company, which pays its president less than the equivalent of $148,000 a year. Mr. Nakauchi's annual income from Daiei (including dividends on his 18 percent stake in its stock) exceeds $3 million.

Mr. Nakauchi is "very aggressive and a person thinking of the destruction of a traditional order," says Yoshihiro Tajima, a professor of economics at Gakushuin University and an expert on retailing.

Source: *Wall Street Journal* (August 2, 1981):1.

for their "American" approach to management and negotiation. (See Exhibit 8-1 for more detail.)

Further, we have witnessed unusual behavior from even the highest ranking Japanese officials. Kazuo Wakasugi, director of MITI's trade policy bureau, has threatened to trade with the communists if Americans and Europeans refuse to trade. Wakasugi was immediately and roundly criticized for his remarks by other Japanese officials, including his boss at MITI.

Not only have we found personality differences to be important in our dealings with Japanese clients, we also have discovered apparent differences in negotiation style based on industry, expatriate experiences, and age.

Negotiation Styles Differ Across Industries in Japan

We have found important differences in negotiation styles across industries in Japan. Perhaps the most dramatic comparison is that between the Japanese banking and retailing industries. Negotiations with Japanese bankers will almost always proceed in the traditional way. However, major retailers in Japan, such as Daiei, Ito Yokado, Seiyu, JUSCO, and UNY seem to take a different approach to strategic decisionmaking. We must point out that more routine or smaller transactions are usually handled in the more traditional ways even when large Japanese retailers are the clients.

For example, we know that in the late 1960s the president of Seiyu Department Stores, against the advice of his middle managers, opened an American subsidiary store in Los Angeles. Such a decision would not happen in the Japanese banking industry. We have learned this lesson through experience. One mistake the authors made a few years ago was to contact directly the president of one of Japan's largest banks about a relatively large American acquisition, a strategy we have found successful in the retailing industry. However, at the bank we were politely but firmly informed that this was not the proper way to conduct business with a Japanese financial institution. So we started over, contacting middle management first.

Generally, the major firms in established industries will negotiate in the traditional way. Smaller firms, particularly if they have been exposed previously to international transactions, and if they are in newer industries, *may* take a more flexible, less traditional approach to business negotiations. But the key word is *may*. The *shokai-sha* will be the most important source of information regarding whether your clients' negotiation styles fit the Japanese stereotype.

Japanese Negotiators with Expatriate Experiences

Japanese with experience living or working in the United States will usually adjust their bargaining style and appear to understand a Western approach. Indeed, we have noticed in our negotiation simulations that Japanese executives living only six months in the United States begin unconsciously to reflect the communication style (eye contact, conversational rhythm) of American bargainers.

But the degree to which these Japanese will understand and respond to the American style of negotiations can differ depending on the length and quality of their stay in America. The answers to simple questions such as, "How long did you spend in the United States?" and "What were your responsibilities there?" will help gauge their understanding. Generally, higher level expatriate tours of duty (such as head of a subsidiary or middle manager) are shorter (three to five years) and involve primarily contact with headquarters personnel in Japan. Alternatively, staff or trainee assignments are for five to six years and entail much more contact with American suppliers and clients. The Japanese with lower level staff experience in the United States can thus be expected to be more familiar with Western negotiation practices.

You should also be aware that most Japanese with such a bicultural competence are able to switch their American style on and off. We have seen such Japanese bargainers, fully capable of forthright responses to key questions, "clam up" and play the role of the typical indirect Japanese.

You are more likely to focus your attention on such executives because they speak English better, they appear to understand you better, and they appear to be smarter. This is a mistake. Often, the Japanese executive with long expatriate experience is the least influential in the group.

Age

Japanese executives to whom we talk often point out a generation gap in their ranks. That is, businessmen educated after World War II have considerably different values and attitudes about life, management, and negotiation. During the postwar occupation Japanese society underwent considerable changes—some mandated by General MacArthur, but primarily dictated by a new exposure to a rapidly changing world. This cadre of younger executives, the oldest of whom are now in their mid-thirties, are commonly described as less traditional, more independent, and more verbal. In fact, all of Japanese youth tends to display more interest in foreign cultures, foreign languages, and international travel. Kazuma Uyeno describes the lost art of *ishin-denshin:*

> *Ishin-denshin* is communication of thought without the medium of words. The expression means "what the mind thinks, the heart transmits." In other societies, particularly Western, communication generally has to be expressed in specific words to be thoroughly understood. To the Westerner, therefore, the Japanese sometimes seem to have telepathic powers because so often communication among Japanese is achieved without the use of words.
>
> This is because the many formalities, conventions and common standards developed in a society which gives priority to harmonious relations makes it easy to understand what goes on in the mind of the other person.
>
> The younger generation of Japanese who have become more individualistic are losing the *ishin-denshin* faculty.[1]

And as in the case with any generation gap, both the older and the younger complain about one another.

This particular generation gap is important for American negotiators to appreciate. Right now these younger executives hold operational staff positions and their influence on decisionmaking styles and negotiation processes is limited. However, beginning in the mid-1980s these younger businesspeople will graduate to the ranks of middle management. It is then that we Americans should expect to see significant changes in the way Japanese handle commercial relationships with foreign firms.

Homogeneity

Obviously we think there is value in describing both the typical American negotiation style and the typical Japanese negotiation style. Although the values and behaviors appear to be very different *within* each of the two cultures, when viewed from outside there appears to be a great deal more homogeneity. This is particularly so when the two cultures are so different. We feel that by better understanding one another's cultures, values, and behaviors we can improve communication and anticipate one another's needs. Such understanding is critical to a mutually satisfying exchange relationship. This is true for individuals, business enterprises, and countries.

RACIAL AND ETHNIC PREJUDICE

Very few countries in the world share America's ideals of racial and ethnic equality. We say "ideals" because sometimes Americans aren't very good at ignoring color and race—as indicated in the excerpt below:

> Is the United States faced with a new "yellow peril?" There is abundant evidence that many Americans think so.
>
> Last year in Milwaukee, a Japanese flag was slashed and stomped on by an angry crowd of U.S. auto workers. In St. Louis, a shipment of Japanese made cars was mysteriously destroyed by bullets and knives. Labor unions have begun to pass out inflammatory literature, crying, "Remember Pearl Harbor." A national tabloid ran a story, reprinted as an advertisement by a major car manufacturer, charging that this country "whipped the Japanese in World War II but now they're getting even by shipping us millions of dangerous cars that kill tens of thousands of Americans every year."
>
> Inflammatory and questionable as such statistics are, more and more politicians are demanding protectionist legislation against Japanese imports. And Gov. Jerry Brown asserted to a group of business leaders last year that Japan poses a more dangerous threat to the United States than does the Soviet Union.
>
> All of which makes the conclusion of syndicated columnist Mark Shields, published in these pages last week, seem an understatement: "If Americans are looking for a political scapegoat this year, Japan may be it."[2]

And it's not just American auto workers that exhibit such racist tendencies. Kim Clark reports that American executives display their distaste for Japanese style management during his seminars on corporate strategy at the Harvard Business School. "You can just see it. They roll their eyes and sort of turn off. The questions I do get are more strident and bitter. To my dismay, there are a lot of racist comments which I had never seen before."[3] Americans that demonstrate this kind of ethnic prejudice will not be successful in Japan. Your Japanese clients will easily read such feelings and business discussion will simply not proceed.

The Japanese aren't any better. In fact, some argue that racial prejudice is a particular problem in Japan because of the history of isolationism and the resulting ethnic homogeneity. And this ethnic homogeneity will certainly persist, given Japan's virtual ban on naturalization of aliens. But our concern here is not social reform. Rather, we must consider how racial and ethnic prejudice influences the efficiency of business negotiations between American and Japanese companies.

Let us begin by saying that Japanese clients expect to deal with American executives who are Caucasian and male. This is their stereotype of "the American business executive." And although many Japanese have trouble handling foreigners in general, they at least know more about Caucasian males, who have earned their respect. After all, Commodore Matthew Perry and General Douglas MacArthur, the two individuals most responsible for westernizing Japan, were Caucasian males.

This expectation and stereotype have caused problems for both Japanese and American executives. Blacks, other Orientals, and even Japanese Americans are assumed by the Japanese to be second-class citizens. For example, we know of one second-generation Japanese American municipal official traveling on business to Japan. He and his younger Caucasian male assistant were greeted at the airport by their Japanese hosts. The Japanese assumed the Japanese American was second in command and treated him accordingly. When they learned otherwise, the Japanese hosts were mortified at their mistake. They had lost face, and much time had to be spent patching things up, including bringing in a new set of hosts. Such a circumstance may seem a bit comical, but the relationship suffered. And in a land where personal relationships are so important, this was a serious problem.

Americans who don't fit the Japanese executive's stereotype may make Japanese clients uncomfortable at first. Black or Oriental American executives traveling to Japan should realize this and anticipate having to work harder at establishing credibility. When minority executives are sent to negotiate with Japanese clients, the Japanese should be notified ahead of time who is coming and who is in charge.

In this respect, too, things are changing in Japan. Younger executives can be expected to have a broader, less prejudiced view of the world and international business. And generally, minority Americans are treated as foreigners first and minorities second. Once the initial surprise is overcome, most Japanese executives will get down to the business of personal relationships and the economics of the deal.

SEXISM

Time recently did a great disservice to women executives interested in international business. In an otherwise well-conceived article on business negotiations in Japan, the journalist reported:

> Experts on Japanese business methods have compiled numerous guidelines for foreign negotiators. One of the first is that women should not be part of any formal talks. "Women are simply not accepted as business equals in Japan," notes a negotiator for a major U.S. electronics firm. Japanese women are all but barred from the management of big companies, and the important after-hours business socializing in Japan is exclusively stag.[4]

It is true that Japanese women are seldom managers, but that does not necessarily mean that American women can't be successful. To the *Time* article Gerry Muir, in a letter to the editors, responded:

> *Time*'s report says women are not accepted as business equals in Japan. That it not always true. I was the Los Angeles creative director for a large Japanese advertising company and feared that my presence might jeopardize the presentation we were making in Japan. My Japanese boss assured me that his colleagues have nothing against women in business so long as the women are not Japanese.[5]

Indeed, we have found the performance of women executives in Japan to be mixed. Exhibit 8-2 is one woman's report of how American women have handled advertising accounts for Japanese

---

Exhibit 8-2. Advertising Women and "The Japanese Problem."

There are layers upon layers of gentle subtleties—"sometimes when they nod and smile, you think that means 'yes'—you work based on the smile and the nod, only to find out that they really meant 'no.' " The Japanese are governed by an ironic politeness.

Sometimes the layers melt and the subtleties give way to a raw reality— "Once, I was the one laying out a new campaign, and I was supposed to be in charge. Now you'd think, being the only woman there, they couldn't

Exhibit 8-2. continued

ignore me. But every question the Japanese had, every comment, was directed to someone else in the room. It was as if I didn't exist."

These experiences are rooted in culture that rarely bends to embrace women—"In Japan, women don't participate in business decisions, so the rules for women simply haven't been defined. What it all boils down to is that the Japanese are not comfortable with women, and when they are not comfortable, they don't do business."

Indeed, many Japanese firms have training programs for U.S.-bound executives to help them adjust to the cultural differences they will face during the typical three-to-five-year stint most spend in their U.S. subsidiaries—specifically, the ability to deal with a business world that sometimes delegates power to women.

It is the desire to adapt, in part, that is beginning to make it possible for women to survive the demands of the Japanese in this evolving advertising climate. When Bill Moreland, then at Dailey & Associates, put Beri Leiberman on the Honda business three years ago as an account executive, one of the Japanese car company's executives pulled Moreland aside. "He laughed and said, 'You've got a lot of nerve putting a woman on this account.' But I told him to give her a chance, and in a month he was coming back saying she was the best hire on the account," says Moreland, now vp/management superviser at BBDO/West.

In this evolutionary relationship, women working with Japanese clients find themselves trying to wade through a whole new set of workplace nuances—to know when to push and when to retreat, to understand that rank and position can ultimately mean more than being a man or a woman. "It took me two years to learn how to play their mental chess game. There is a tremendous sense of your position in the company, and if the other people in the agency make your position clear, it is my experience that the Japanese will respect it," says one female account executive working with a Japanese client.

A high-ranking American executive who has spent the last 10 years in a Japanese-owned firm observes that "When the orientation is heavily skewed to Japanese hands-on management of the company, women are tolerated. The politeness is always there, but they probably wouldn't take a woman seriously. The same suggestions from a man would be given a lot more consideration. It's better than it was 10 years ago, but many Japanese companies have made no internal transition to include women."

Source: Betsy Sharkoy, "Advertising Women and the Japanese Problem," *Adweek* (May 1983): 32–33.

companies. Further, Nancy Adler, a professor of Management at McGill University in Montreal, found that North American women executives are successfully managing relationships with Japanese clients. She echoes the idea that American women are first foreigners and second women, and they interact with Japanese managers as such. It is true that they don't fit into the traditional routine of golf, Ginza nightclubs, and bath houses but with time they are accepted because of their professional expertise.

The managerial implication here is the same as in the previous section on racial and ethnic prejudice. When women travel to Japan, they must anticipate the attitudes of their clients. With patience and an understanding of the Japanese women can be effective.

Business negotiations across cultures are difficult undertakings, particularly in such a fast-changing world. Much can go wrong besides the economics of the deal. In this chapter we have tried to address the most delicate but very real problems of cultures meeting—personalities, prejudices, and sexism. We don't have all the answers because all the rules haven't yet been established. But we hope to have made you aware of these important, but hidden, pitfalls of business negotiations with the Japanese.

NOTES TO CHAPTER 8

1. Kazuma Uyeno, *Japanese Business Glossary* (Tokyo: Mitsubishi Corporation, Toyo-Keizai-Shinposha, 1983).
2. *Los Angeles Herald Examiner*, March 23, 1982.
3. From "Japan's Strategies May Need Some Tuning To Work Here," *Los Angeles Times*, January 23, 1983, Part IV, p. 3.
4. *Time*, August 1, 1983, p. 42.
5. Gerry Muir, *Time*, August 22, 1983, p. 2.

9 EXPERIENCES OF FOUR AMERICAN COMPANIES

In this chapter we report the experiences of four American companies negotiating with Japanese firms. The four case histories were picked to demonstrate the variety of trans-Pacific business dealings and the mixed performance of American and Japanese negotiators. All four examples illustrate the importance of several of our recommendations made throughout the book.

We begin with a discussion of the unfolding relationship between the two largest automobile manufacturers in the world, General Motors and Toyota. Next, we focus on the several differences evident in an international acquisition negotiation, Fuji Bank's purchase of Walter E. Heller International. Third, we consider the recent bargaining between the Los Angeles Olympic Organizing Committee and the Japanese media regarding broadcasting rights for Japan. Finally, we present the recent successes of Rolm Corporation selling telecommunications systems in Japan with the approval of Nippon Telegraph and Telephone.

THE GENERAL MOTORS–TOYOTA JOINT VENTURE

Japanese automobile manufacturers were pressured by the U.S. government to more quickly build plants in the United States when

Exhibit 9-1. Chronology of the Toyota-GM Joint Venture Negotiation.	
July 2, 1981	Eiji Toyoda, then president of Toyota Motor Corporation, announces discontinuance of negotiation with Ford Motors.
Dec. 21, 1981	Exploratory meeting between Seishi Kato, then the chairman of the board of Toyota Motor Sales, Inc., and Roger Smith, chairman of the board of General Motors.
March 1, 1982	Eiji Toyoda meets with Roger Smith in New York to discuss the possibility of cooperation in small-car production in the United States.
Apr. 14-16, 1982	Jack Smith, director of GM, International Production Planning and other team members of GM visit Toyota Motor Company headquarters; beginning of the first operational level negotiations with Toyota.
May 17-20, 1982	Jack Smith and others hold second operational level negotiation.
June 7-10, 1982	Survey delegation headed by Toshio Morita, executive vice-president of Toyota, visits the United States and reviews a number of GM plants.
June-Sept., 1982	Number of negotiations between them results in a fundamental agreement in areas of type of cars, number of cars to be produced, plant location, and sales channel used to sell the cars.
Sept. 20-23, 1982	GM delegation headed by Jack Smith visits Japan again. Experienced deadlock (difficulty) in areas of plant asset valuation, license fee, and price of cars produced.
Nov. 29, 1982	Eiji Toyoda announces at the Narita International Airport after his trip to the States that they will not be able to reach an agreement by the end of year.
Early Dec. 1982	Roger Smith writes a letter to Eiji Toyoda that GM is willing to soften its stand in plant valuation and urges Toyota to agree.
Dec. 23, 1982	Shigenobu Yamamoto, vice-chairman, and Mananori Iwasaki, managing director, visit Roger Smith in Detroit and exchange views on labor problems. The negotiation difficulty is overcome.

Exhibit 9-1. continued	
Jan. 20-26, 1983	GM delegation headed by Jack Smith visits Japan and begins drafting a letter of understanding of the joint venture company.
Feb. 14, 1983	Formal announcement of the signing of the contract is made.
Feb. 17, 1983	Eiji Toyoda and Roger Smith sign the memorandum of understanding at the GM Fremont plant.

Source: "Mega-Joint Venture Begins to Move Forward: Toyota, GM," *Nihon Keizai Shimbun* (February 16, 1983): 2.

Japanese imports surged to a U.S. market share more than 20 percent. Honda Motors was the first to announce selecting a plant site in Ohio, and they now assemble Accord subcompacts there. Nissan produces pickup trucks in Tennessee.

Growing protectionist sentiment and continuing pressure on voluntarily restraining the Japanese exports to the United States forced Toyota to consider working with Ford Motors in the United States. However, Eiji Toyoda, then president of Toyota Motor Co., announced discontinuation of the negotiations with Ford in July 1981. Shortly thereafter Masayuki Kato, chairman of Toyota Motor Sales, Inc. (the marketing arm of Toyota), formally opened the dialogue between Toyota and GM. Of course, prior to these formal explorations by the top executives of Toyota Motor Sales, Inc., extensive *nemawashi* had taken place. After a series of negotiations on both sides of the Pacific (Exhibit 9-1), General Motors and Toyota agreed to form a joint venture to build 200,000 subcompact cars a year.

The "memorandum of understanding," initialed February 17, 1983, by General Motors and Toyota, requires the creation of an equally owned company to produce front-wheel-drive subcompacts starting in the spring of 1985 for sale via the GM dealer network. General Motors will contribute a Fremont, California assembly plant that was idled in March 1982 and $11 to $20 million in cash; Toyota will contribute $150 million in cash to cover the project's estimated $300 million price tag. Most of the money is to be used for improvements at the Fremont plant, including construction of a stamping plant nearby.

General Motors and Toyota appointed the same number of members to the new firm's board of directors. However, Toyota named the president and chief executive officer, Tatsuro Toyoda, managing director of Toyota Motor Corporation, to run the plant. A crucial aspect of the joint venture was the cooperation of the United Auto Workers (UAW) union. Bill Usery, a former U.S. Labor Secretary, was hired as a consultant to Toyota and GM to negotiate with the UAW, and the labor agreement was reached in September 1983.

Toyota will provide, and receive a royalty for, the design and engineering for the joint venture's car. It also will supply the engines, transaxles, and some other major components for the cars, which will have a 50 percent domestic content. About 3,000 people will be employed at the assembly plant, and up to 9,000 jobs could be generated in supplier firms. General Motors and Toyota each will be entitled to 50 percent of the joint venture's profits.

Lessons

There are several lessons implied in our brief description of the GM–Toyota negotiations. First, the important roles of *shokai-sha* (in this case the trading company) and *nemawashi* (the preliminary meetings) are demonstrated. Second, notice the power relationship—Toyota courting GM and Eiji Toyoda traveling to New York. Next, the roles of the two top executives are illustrated—the *aisatsu* to get things started (March 1982), negotiations moved back to the top to break a deadlock (November–December 1982), and the signing ceremony (February 1983). Fourth, notice Toyota's (unintentional?) use of the media and public opinion to put pressure on Smith. Finally, consider the timing of Yamamoto and Iwasaki's visit to Detroit—right before Christmas (a subtle imposition of a time limit?).

Overall, we feel that the negotiation was successful because both sides managed the bargaining process adroitly. Obviously, both had much to gain from cooperation, but economics aren't enough to make a business relationship work. Patience, attention to detail, and adaptation of negotiation styles are also important.

FUJI BANK ACQUIRES HELLER
INTERNATIONAL

In our experience, merger and acquisition negotiations involving Japanese firms often break with the normal negotiation and decision-making styles we have described throughout the book. In particular, such negotiations often move much faster, involve fewer Japanese executives, and focus on tangible assets rather than long-term profits and cash flows. We develop these three points in more detail below.

During the past few years several Japanese banks with U.S. subsidiaries have acquired independent California banks. Sanwa Bank of California purchased Golden State Bank (eleven branches), effective January 31, 1978, for $25.3 million. Subsequently, the name was changed to Golden State Sanwa Bank. In early 1981 Mitsubishi Bank, Ltd. acquired First National Bank of San Diego County (ten branches) for $26.5 million and, later, the Bank of California (one of the ten largest California banks, the Rothchilds being a major stockholder). Also in July 1981 Mitsui Bank, Ltd. took over Manufacturer's Bank, thirteenth largest in the state, for $173 million; the new name is Mitsui Manufacturer's Bank, now ranked twelfth in California. The negotiations between Mitsui and Manufacturer's lasted approximately five months, and a letter of understanding was written in November 1980.

Following this trend of Japanese investment in the United States is Fuji Bank's (Japan's second-largest financial institution) acquisition of Walter E. Heller International for $425 million. Part of the story was told in the *Economist:*

This is the largest direct investment ever made by a Japanese company in América. In the 30 years to March 31, 1982, Japanese direct investment in banking and insurance in North America amounted to $1.4 billion. This does not include a share of the $82 million spent by Japanese companies on setting up and expanding branch offices. Over the same period, total Japanese investment in all sectors in North America topped $12.3 billion.

If the deal goes through, Fuji Bank will become the new owner of two subsidiaries of Walter E. Heller International. These are Walter E. Heller (which has assets of $2.8 billion, a net worth of $360m and is one of America's many concerns specializing in commercial loans, leases and factoring), and

Walter E. Heller Overseas. This has subsidiaries and joint ventures in more than 20 countries abroad. Its net worth is $31m and total assets are $700m.

Like other leading Japanese banks, Fuji was approached by the American parent company last November. Fuji was interested from the start and has stuck throughout to is original offer of $425m. That is $25m more than Security Pacific offered in a tentative rival offer.

Heller International terminated its letter of intent with Security Pacific when Mr. Ko Uemura, a senior managing director of Fuji Bank, flew to Tokyo and persuaded the Japanese ministry of finance to lift the requirement to obtain its formal approval before the deal could be clinched.

The Fuji deal may set a new fashion for the way Japanese banks break into the American market. Hitherto, banks like Sumitomo and the Bank of Tokyo got their foot in the door by buying banks in California. Japanese banks have also established branch offices and trust-type operations in New York. This acquisition, however, will give the Japanese a business network throughout America. If they had pounced on a bank, they would be limited to operating in one state as American banking law now stands. If interstate banking is approved, the Heller finance operations could be turned into a nationwide banking network.

Meanwhile, Fuji says it wants to expand into the leasing and factoring business and needs an introduction to the more profitable financing business for small and medium-sized companies.

Fuji Bank has hitherto been frustrated in attempts to broaden its large industrial clientele through participation in syndicated loans initiated by multinational American banks. It wanted access to companies with assets of $200m or less.

Walter E. Heller and its overseas corporation employ $3.5 billion in assets to purchase corporate receivables at a discount, lease equipment, and other sophisticated asset-base financing. However, Heller's profitability was reduced by the recession to only $10m last year, down from roughly $30m in a good year. It has an above-average $360m in non-earning "assets."[1]

What is so remarkable about Fuji's move is that they had gathered extensive information prior to the time Walter Heller approached them. They had asked one of the more well-known American research institutes to identify the recent and future environment of the banking and financial markets in the United States. The recommendation was to acquire a nonbank financial institution such as Walter Heller. By the time Walter Heller's investment bankers approached Fuji, the executives were already prepared to make a decision.

Although the Japanese in most situations will make decisions by consensus, slowly, and at their own pace, in acquisitions such as the Fuji–Walter Heller deal, they can act swiftly. It's true that Fuji had decided beforehand to look for such a company as Walter Heller, but even so, their securing the deal within six months after the opportunity surfaced is surprising. The Fuji people knew that if things moved too slowly, other suitors would arrive on the scene.

Another aspect of acquisition negotiations that is inconsistent with the Japanese negotiation style regards secrecy. In the United States, usually only a few top executives are informed about acquisition or merger talks. The same is often true of Japanese companies—acquisition decisions tend to be much more top-down than in other kinds of business deals. The information and analysis is handled by a small group of top executives to maintain confidentiality. The normal *ringi-sho* (consensus decisionmaking document) is often eliminated. Finally, it should be noted that this break with the traditional negotiation and decisionmaking style is less common in the more traditional sectors of Japanese industry. That is, more people and more management levels will be involved in the decisionmaking in banks than in other businesses such as retailing. But even there, fewer executives will be involved in merger and acquisition decisions.

Finally, acquisition negotiations with the Japanese will not follow the expected pattern because of their unusual view of company valuation. We mentioned that one of the basic differences between Americans and Japanese concerned Japanese executives' long planning horizon for business deals. We suggested that Japanese clients will be interested in the viability of potential business relationships well into the 1990s. Such is not the case for acquisitions. Where Americans value future cash flows, Japanese consider almost exclusively present assets. The Japanese tend to focus on tangible assets such as land and real properties. The value of a company depends on how many branches the company has and how many are leased or owned. They won't be as interested in the presentation of estimates of future income streams. The fact that a company earns say $10 million per year with a small asset base does not mean that the company is worth $80 million (assuming a continuous future income flow and today's 12 percent plus interest rates). Instead, the Japanese will be interested in the worth of that small asset base—a short-term view indeed.

LOS ANGELES OLYMPIC ORGANIZING
COMMITTEE (LAOOC) AND THE
JAPANESE MEDIA

In late 1982, *Nippon Hoso Kyokai* (NHK), Japan's government-owned TV broadcasting company, called on LAOOC to purchase broadcasting rights for the 1984 Olympics. The negotiations got off to a difficult start when NHK offered $6 million and LAOOC countered with $90 million.

The Japanese viewed the first offer as a "banana sale" tactic. However, the Americans provided a reasonable explanation: Japan has the highest number of color televisions per capita in the world. ABC had "happily" paid $225 million to broadcast the games in the United States (that's about $1.60 for each American household). So $90 million wasn't an unreasonable demand given Japan's population of more than 115 million. Moreover, the Americans felt they were in a good bargaining position—Japan, like the United States, did not broadcast the Moscow games in 1980; thus, Japanese viewers would insist on seeing Olympics this time around.

However, a major difference in the market structure of the countries weighed heavily on the negotiations. LAOOC had at least three potential customers in the United States—ABC, NBC, and CBS. In Japan they could only sell to NHK (noncommercial TV). The bilateral monopoly conditions forced LAOOC to reevaluate its asking price. After several visits by the Japanese negotiators and meetings in Luzon and Rome, the negotiations stalled, LAOOC asking $19 million, NHK making a final offer of $18 million (the maximum approved by their home office). The deadlock was finally broken by splitting the difference and agreeing to a price of $18.5 million. The Japanese justified the extra half million to their home office by explaining that the purchase also included rights to pre-Olympic broadcasts during the summer of 1983.

After an agreement was reached on price, LAOOC made a surprise demand regarding the terms of payment. They wanted the $18.5 immediately, in January 1983. The NHK representatives had not anticipated such a demand. They calculated that the interest LAOOC would make (and NHK would lose) during 1983 would be more than $2 million. The Japanese would have preferred to bargain over price and terms simultaneously, trading off the two issues. They made a major concession by agreeing to pay on February 19, 1983.

The Japanese bargainers described LAOOC negotiators as formidable bargainers. They used several tactics to their advantage. First, the $90 million price tag, with the reasonable explanation, softened up the Japanese side considerably. Second, Peter Ueberroth, head of the LAOOC negotiating team, indicated that all decisions and concessions were made by the committee; he was there only to listen. This consensus decisionmaking style is uncharacteristic for Americans and was not anticipated by the Japanese. Next, the Americans appeared to use a "good guy, bad guy" tactic. Ueberroth often sympathized with the Japanese, but Harry L. Usher, the LAOOC executive vice-president and general manager, took a decidedly hard-headed approach and was always the last one to be convinced. One might say Ueberroth maintained the *wa* while Usher made the tough demands.

The experience of the LAOOC negotiators also made a difference. All were experienced negotiators with legal backgrounds. Further, Ueberroth was an experienced international negotiator; he had previously successfully managed a travel agency with worldwide operations. Because of the LAOOC negotiation team's complete preparations and familiarity with the Japanese style of bargaining, they were able to anticipate the various strategies of the NHK team.

While the LAOOC team used their experience to their advantage, the NHK representatives had varied backgrounds. One was the chief news correspondent for NHK in Los Angeles (a professional reporter). Another was the director in charge of Olympic coverage for the Japanese audience. Because no professional negotiators were involved on the NHK side, the Americans were more apt to trust the Japanese representatives. The credibility of the Japanese explanations was a key factor in moving LAOOC from $90 million to $18.5 million.

Although Michael O'Hara of the LAOOC indicated their original goal to be $10 million, all in all, neither side was completely satisfied with the outcome. The Olympic Committee had hoped for even more revenue from the NHK contract. The Japanese felt they were forced to make large concessions and had to go to great pains to sell the deal to their headquarters. Despite each side's expectations about the deal, the Americans appear to have moved the Japanese as far as possible by using their good understanding of the Japanese negotiation style. A short review of the tactics used by LAOOC is appropriate:

1. Making large initial demands and having reasonable explanations for them;

2. Making concessions based on bilateral monopoly conditions and sincerity of Japanese;
3. Using creativity regarding inclusion of pre-Olympic broadcasts;
4. Using creativity regarding terms of payment;
5. Negotiating *without* authority—decisions were made by LAOOC;
6. Using a "good-guy, bad-guy" routine—Ueberroth maintained *wa* while Usher applied pressure;
7. The presence of Ueberroth, with his international experience and knowledge of the Japanese bargaining style.

ROLM CORPORATION AND NTT

In the following excerpt from his *Los Angeles Times* article, Michael S. Malone describes the details of a most interesting trans-Pacific business negotiation.

In light of recent trade tensions between the United States and Japan, notably in the arena of high technology, one recent case stands out as an example of how American firms, with attention to detail and almost unbelievable patience, can penetrate the Japanese home market.

The success story involves Rolm Corp., a $400-million manufacturer of computerized telephone PBX systems based in Santa Clara, in California's Silicon Valley, and its negotiations with giant Nippon Telephone & Telegraph Corp., the AT&T of Japan. In March, 1982, after three years of seemingly glacial progress, Nippon Telephone approved Rolm's proposal to sell its products in Japan, connected to the Nippon Telephone system. This certification made Rolm the first approved supplier of digital switching systems in Japan—beating out even native competitors such as Nippon Electric, Hitachi, Fujitsu and Oki.

Rolm estimates that by 1985 sales of Rolm equipment in Japan may exceed $50 million.

"It wasn't really that difficult," says Wolfgang H. Schwarz, general manager of Rolm's International Telecommunications division. "It wasn't a coup, or anything like that, because when you get right down to it, selling in Japan is just like selling in Australia or Italy.

"The myth I want to dispel is that to deal with the Japanese you have to be a great strategist or a great negotiator."

In April, 1979, while on a selling tour of the Far East, Schwarz decided to stop in Tokyo and pay a visit to Nippon Telephone. The Japanese company had never allowed a digital switching system to be interconnected to its network, permitting only the traditional electromechanical type, and Schwarz was curious to know why—and perhaps drum up a little business. His goal was not only to gain approval to sell Rolm digital PBXs to Nippon Telephone, but, more important, to obtain "type" approval to sell the equipment to *any* customer in Japan and be able to interconnect to the Japanese network.

Schwarz, who had in the past worked for firms in Hong Kong and Kenya, was not afraid to make a "cold" call. He simply showed up unannounced at the front desk of multibillion-dollar Nippon Telephone and told the security guard he wanted to talk to someone in charge of buying PBX systems. PBX, or private branch exchange, refers to a telephone switchboard system operating within a building or company that has outside telephone lines.

It took two days to be pushed up the chain of command, but Schwarz was finally allowed to meet with the company director of strategic planning. "Not much came out of that meeting," Schwarz says. The director explained why Nippon Telephone didn't have digital systems and that the firm was looking into the technology. The director also offered to supply Schwarz with all the specifications for Nippon Telephone's electromechanical systems in hopes that they would provide him with some insight into how the Nippon Telephone telecommunications network worked.

Schwarz happily accepted the material, thanked the director and returned home. In retrospect, Schwarz says he found the Nippon Telephone executive as straightforward as any he had dealt with in the Far East—there was no sign of subtle trade barriers being quietly erected to stop Rolm.

The next year, Schwarz says, "was the fun part" of the negotiations, mainly because they weren't yet weighed down with details. Schwarz made half a dozen trips to Japan. These trips had two objectives: To put together an effective distribution network in expectation of eventual success and to continue to convince Nippon Telephone of the value of digital equipment.

By the end of the year, the distribution network was in place and ready, with Sumitomo Corp. as Rolm's trading partner and Omron Tateishi Electronics Co. handling sales and service.

The negotiations with Nippon Telephone were also moving smoothly, if imperceptibly, forward. Most of the time, Schwarz says, these meetings took place in the evening, over dinner at an old-fashioned restaurant, at which both sides carefully tested the waters through great tact and carefully orchestrated ceremony.

Hours of Preparation

"The Japanese executive puts in a 5½-to-6-day workweek, with 12-hour days. So a workday often ends with dinner meeting lasting until 11 at night." And these dinner meetings require as much preparations as one during the day, Schwarz adds. He says he often spent two hours beforehand carefully whittling down his thoughts to a few key questions. He knew that the gentleman sitting across the table would have made the same preparations. During these early meetings, the Japanese questions revolved around Rolm and the American telecommunications industry. Schwarz's questions tried to ferret out what the eventual Nippon Telephone digital specifications would be.

"To the Japanese, change comes in small degrees," Schwarz says. "You need to set up everything long beforehand, so on D-Day all the aspects come together harmoniously."

Yet, despite all this ceremony, Schwarz is convinced that the average American businessman can succeed quite well at these meetings with certain preparations regarding the business discussions (learn their names, and make sure no one loses face when you discuss a problem) and standard, polite American table manners.

"Of course," he adds, "if you're dealing with a U.S.-educated Japanese executive, you can throw all the ceremony right out the window, because what he wants to know is who's going to be in Alabama's football lineup next year."

Trade Secrets at Issue

A second problem was that Nippon Telephone wanted to know about the structure of the software used in the Rolm digital PBX—the key to Rolm's competitiveness. "We weren't prepared to give it to them," Schwarz says. But at the same time he didn't want to risk their anger by saying no. So Schwarz tried a different tack: He pointed out to Nippon Telephone that the Australian telecommunications system, one of the most admired in the world, had never felt the need to ask for such information.

It worked; the Japanese withdrew their questions.[2]

We contacted Mr. Schwarz at the Rolm offices in Santa Clara to see if he had any comments regarding the *Times* article. He was happy to report that Rolm had recently announced the sale of a $2 million PBX system to Japan Airlines. He added that since the NTT approval, things were going well for his company in Japan with sales of thirty to thirty five systems . . . in process." He also mentioned that he felt that the *Times* reporter "overplayed" the importance of the dinner meetings. "They were important, but most of the technical discussions were at NTT offices." We asked him about the cold call he had made on NTT, since this seemed highly unusual based on our own experiences in Japan. Mr. Schwarz explained that cold calls were his trademark—"You can learn a great deal about how a company works by starting at the front desk and working your way up."

The *Times* article is an excellent one. It demonstrates Mr. Schwarz's skills of negotiation which led to Rolm's success. We must take exception, however, to some of Schwarz's comments and tactics. Although we agree that you don't have to be a superman to sell in Japan, you must understand what makes Japan different from most other countries in the world, including Australia and Italy. We also feel that the primary reason Schwarz's cold call routine achieved any results had to do with NTT's recent heightened consciousness of Americans' trade barrier criticisms.

Schwarz and his negotiation team get our highest praise for asking questions, being patient, and putting up with the necessary ceremony. Further, his indirect refusal to answer questions about proprietary technology was most insightful. Finally, the Rolm team checked frequently with their NTT peers as they developed the necessary documentation for the specifications. As Schwarz points out, such close communications between Rolm and NTT operational level managers was the key to winning approval.

In sum, except for the cold call, we applaud Schwarz's handling of the negotiations with NTT, a tough customer indeed. If other American firms follow Rolm's good example, sales of American high tech products to Japan will continue to increase.

NOTES TO CHAPTER 9

1. "Breaking Wide in America," *Economist* (March 28, 1983): 100.
2. Michael S. Malone, "How a Santa Clara Firm Sold High Tech to Japan," *Los Angeles Times*, March 25, 1983, Business Section, p. 1.

10 A SUMMARY OF PRESCRIPTIONS FOR AMERICANS

This chapter is composed of a summary list of prescriptions for Americans bargaining in Japan. It is best used for refreshing your memory before your next negotiation in Japan. We have written it to be easily read at some point during your next nine- to twelve-hour flight across the Pacific. It summarizes the key points from Chapters 4 through 7.

Chapter 11 may be of particular interest to you. There we present a similar summary list of prescriptions for Japanese executives traveling to the United States. You may be interested to learn what problems the American style poses for Japanese executives.

COMMENTS OF WALTER BERAN

Before reviewing our recommendations from the earlier chapters, we feel it may be insightful to consider the advice and comments of Walter Beran, an experienced and successful negotiator in Japan.

Walter Beran is the former chairman of the Los Angeles Area Chamber of Commerce and presently vice-chairman of Ernst & Whinney, a big eight accounting firm. Business with Japanese clients has taken him to Japan frequently. Most recently he was invited by the Ministry of International Trade and Industry (MITI) and the

Japan External Trade Organization (JETRO) for a series of informal talks with Japanese industrial and political leaders. During the trip he met with Shintaro Abe, then head of MITI, and Masumi Esaki, a leader in the Liberal Democratic party, to discuss the Japan–U.S. trade relationship.

We asked Beran to suggest the most important considerations for Americans negotiating with Japanese clients or partners. His response was as follows:

> Preparation before the talks begin is imperative. You and/or your staff should gather and analyze as much financial and personal background information as possible. Your Japanese clients will have carefully prepared and you put yourself at great disadvantage if your haven't done likewise. The advice and comments of others who have dealt with your Japanese clients previously will be most helpful. For example, before my meetings with officials at MITI, I was briefed by executives of the American Chamber of Commerce in Japan. They provided me with insight regarding the topics of conversation to expect — both commercial and personal. Because of the extent of our preparations the meetings at MITI went well. However, you should also realize that even given the best preparations, things usually arise that you haven't anticipated. Flexibility is key.

Beran also emphasized the importance of taking assistants (*kaban-mochi*) on trips to Japan:

> An assistant can help in several ways. He or she can be given responsibilities for managing detailed technical and commercial information. He will also be a big help in reviewing and interpreting meeting outcomes. Another pair of ears and eyes can make a big difference in learning about the needs and preferences of your clients. An assistant will be particularly helpful informally, making arrangements and talking with lower level Japanese executives. His presence will also communicate to the Japanese the importance of your visit and your commitment to the business relationship. Finally, an assistant that [*sic*] speaks Japanese will be doubly helpful in understanding the Japanese reactions, verbal and nonverbal, and in providing guidance regarding business etiquette and protocol.
>
> Interpreters also must be used wisely. The natural thing to do when using an interpreter is to look at him while he speaks and as you speak to him. This is a mistake. It's important that you give your attention to the Japanese executive, even during the interpretation process. Even a novice can pick up important information without a knowledge of nonverbal signals peculiar to the Japanese. In my talks with one of the key ministers of the

government, I knew my time was about up when his secretary brought in a message. I summed things up and was ready to leave in five minutes.

Beran believes the first thing to be done in meetings with groups of Japanese executives is figure out who's their top man. This will be particularly important because during the meeting most of the conversation should be focused on him. It will make you feel a bit uncomfortable to ignore the lower level executives present, but it's the Japanese way. You should always know, before the meeting begins, who their top man is. But it's also easy to tell because the Japanese group will be introduced in order of rank, highest first.

> Beran also spoke about the need for self-control in Japan. You should try to be quiet and reserved in Japan. Let them do the talking. It's a tough thing to do, and it takes practice. All of us have the urge to swoop in, like an eagle with talons open and seize a conversational advantage. But I've found that with Japanese clients it's best to keep your talons hidden.
>
> Status in Japan is critical. You should subtly flaunt your title and position if you think it will give you an advantage. It's not our style, but it can help if you have your assistant treat you with extra deference and respect during meetings with Japanese. This role playing will add to your status with your Japanese clients.

Beran further cautioned that the work doesn't end when the negotiations are over. "I've found it most useful to take some time immediately following meetings to review and analyze the process and outcomes. Even if I don't have a lot of time, I'll dictate my thoughts and impressions into my cassette recorder immediately for follow-up."

Beran summarized his recommendations by saying, "all you need is to be extremely well prepared, extra alert, studious, flexible, yet reserved in negotiations with your Japanese clients. Sprinkle all of these with patience as you strive for a successful conclusion. Your *kabanmochi* should be more competent than you."

SELECTION OF NEGOTIATION TEAMS
(Chapter 4)

One of the most important points we have tried to make concerns negotiation team composition. Taking along "extras" isn't consistent with the American negotiation style. Consequently, we are usually outnumbered in our negotiations with Japanese clients. This is a mistake for several reasons.

1. The Japanese negotiation team will consist of three levels of executives, each with a different role in the negotiations. Top executives are there for ceremony. Middle managers are there to "bless" intermediate agreements. Operational staff executives are there to negotiate (in the American sense). It will be most difficult for a lone American negotiator to play all three roles, each requiring a different set of behaviors.

2. The Japanese will ask for detailed technical information. It will be difficult for one American to both handle the all-important personal relationships and manage the large volume of technical information exchanged.

3. Perhaps the single most important reason for sending at least two executives to negotiate with Japanese clients has to do with the lower level, informal channel of communication. Your lower level executive should be assigned the responsibility of obtaining information from the Japanese that would not ordinarily be communicated at the negotiation table. The same channel should also be used for delivering the more aggressive persuasive appeals. Bringing along someone to manage this informal channel is absolutely essential for efficient Japanese-American negotiations.

4. Negotiation includes overt and covert social pressures. Subtleties like nodding heads and positive facial expressions can be powerful influences on negotiation outcomes. Negotiation is a social activity, and the approval and agreement of others can mean the difference between success and failure.

5. Numbers can be an indicator of the seriousness and commitment of both parties to a mutually beneficial business relationship.

We suggest that in negotiations with Japanese you use team assistance wisely. Don't hesitate to include additional members on your team such as financial or technical experts. The extra expense may be an excellent investment. Also, observation of negotiations can be a valuable training experience for younger members of the organization. Even if they add little to the discussion, their presence may make a difference. They should be assigned listening responsibilities and management of the informal channel of communication.

Often it will be necessary to include an interpreter on your negotiation team. Be sure to brief and debrief this valuable source of information. Be conscious of quality; you get what you pay for. Specialists are available for government, engineering, or financial discussions.

We have identified seven bargainer characteristics that you should look for in representatives to be sent overseas. They are:

1. Listening ability;
2. Interpersonal orientation—someone who is responsive to your client's or partner's approach to negotiation, someone who is flexible;
3. Willingness to use team assistance;
4. High self-esteem—belief in one's ideas and abilities;
5. High aspirations—someone who has high expectations regarding the business deal;
6. Attractiveness—someone who can make other people interested and comfortable;
7. Influence at headquarters—half the negotiation is with the home office.

We also said that when selecting representatives for business with Japanese clients you should look for two additional characteristics: patience and reticence. Do not send someone who is aggressive, impatient, and a fervent debater. Moreover, do not select someone who displays strong ethnocentrism. Such characteristics will lead to failure when your clients are Japanese.

The best way to make judgments about such bargainer characteristics is through observation of the prospective representatives in action—either a real or a simulated business negotiation. Lacking an opportunity for observation of negotiators, an interview is best. Prospective representatives should be asked to assess their own characteristics and interviewers should look for signs of the critical characteristics described above.

Finally, recognize the importance of a good introduction in Japan. *Shokai-sha* will make things move faster in trans-Pacific business transactions.

NEGOTIATION PRELIMINARIES
(Chapter 5)

Preparation for meetings with Japanese clients or partners includes two aspects. First, gathering information and planning strategies and tactics will be important. Second, manipulation of the negotiation situation—location, timing, and so on—may have a dramatic impact on the negotiation process and outcomes. The best negotiators on both sides of the Pacific manage such details with great care. To get the most out of business negotiations it is important to have every causal factor working in your favor. The time spent in careful planning and detailed adjustment of situational factors is an important investment.

Efficient preparations are best accomplished using the following six-point checklist:

1. *Assessment of the People and the Situation.* Much can be learned about your Japanese clients through readily available information sources. Financial and marketing data, lists of potential distributors, and appropriate *shokai-sha* can be found by reference to the various resources listed in the Appendix. And you must know whom you are to be bargaining with in Japan. Biographical information that will be useful during nontask sounding can be found in the Japanese executives' "Who's Who" (*Shinshiroku*). Beyond these public records you should consult with other American executives who have dealt with the Japanese company in the past. *Shokai-sha* may also be able to provide both economic and personal details otherwise not readily available. Finally, we strongly recommend that you try to assess all this information from the Japanese point of view as well as your own. For example, where your company is considering a three-year planning horizon, your Japanese counterparts are probably looking at least ten years down the road.

2. *Facts to Confirm During the Negotiation.* You and your negotiation team should compose a list of key assumptions and facts to be confirmed at the negotiation table. No matter how well you prepare, things will be different once the talks begin. Expect change and/or inaccuracies, even in the most carefully gathered

information. Go through your checklist with your clients at the beginning.

3. *Agenda.* Write out your agenda. Check it with your Japanese counterparts before the discussion. Follow the agenda and don't make concessions on any issue until all have been discussed.

4. *Best Alternative to a Negotiated Agreement (BATNA).* Your BATNA is your source of power in negotiations. No matter how large your client, if you have a good alternative *and* you know about it, then you have power. If you have no strategic alternative, then you're setting yourself up for an unpleasant experience. If you have done a good job in assessing the people and the situation, then you understand the market for your products, services, or company. That understanding is the key to power.

5. *Concession Strategies.* It's important that you write these strategies out. Never split the difference! Make concessions only after breaks, during which you can consult your preplanned and documented concession strategies. All members of the negotiation team should work together to stay with the plan. The social and time pressures of important business negotiations can be powerful, so it's important to plan this part of the process carefully.

6. *Team Assignments.* Find out who the Japanese are sending. Structure your team accordingly. Make certain everyone understands their responsibilities and role—top executives for ceremony, bottom executives for informal bargaining, and so on.

Seven aspects of the negotiation situation should be manipulated, ahead of time, to your company's advantage. These issues may seem trivial, but the best negotiators pay attention to such details. Apparently minor considerations can make a major difference. The situational factors are:

1. *Location.* Have them come to you if at all possible. If you have the "home court" advantage then you have information more readily available. You don't have to stay in a hotel, you have more people available, and you have the perceived power of being able to summon others. In Japan this power dimension is even more important. When an impasse is reached regarding location, Hawaii is a good neutral location. And in the event that you

do travel to Japan, you might suggest holding meetings at your hotel.

2. *Physical Arrangements.* If you travel to Japan, your prospective business partners will handle the physical arrangements and you should expect formality. If you wish to make your Japanese clients feel comfortable in the United States, then formality is the rule. "Just call me John" may make you feel more relaxed, but it has the opposite effect on most Japanese executives.

3. *Number of Parties.* Resist the temptation to get everyone together and hammer out an agreement. Instead, we advise a *nemawashi* or lobbying approach. Meet with the trading company representatives separately from the government officials and separately from the client.

4. *Number of Participants.* Don't go it alone. There's simply too much going on, particularly in a negotiation with Japanese executives — ceremony and hard bargaining, formal and informal talks, technical details, and financial calculations. Take along at least one other to help. They will at worst receive valuable training and at best add an important dimension to the negotiation process.

5. *Audiences.* Consider the audiences in the GM–Toyota deal: other suitors, governments, public opinion, unions, and related competitors. How might such audiences help or hurt you? It's important that you consider these questions because certainly your Japanese clients will.

6. *Channels of Communication.* Face-to-face negotiations are required with Japanese partners. Letters are also useful for follow-up communications, but telephones and telex are usually used for saying no in Japan. Personal relationships, the key to business relationships in Japan, can only be established through extended periods of face-to-face contact.

7. *Time Limits.* Know your time limits. And just as important, understand theirs. Also understand that the Japanese clock ticks more slowly than the American clock. They are looking for a long-term relationship and will not rush into anything. They would rather miss out on an opportunity than risk a bad decision. Time will generally be on the Japanese negotiators' side, unless you give careful consideration to their time limits. Also,

you will need to make your headquarters understand how things are different in Japan. Your patience and your superiors' patience will be tested, but it's critical that you don't place unnecessary constraints on your own time.

AT THE NEGOTIATION TABLE
(Chapter 6)

The most difficult aspect of an international business negotiation is the actual conduct of the face-to-face meeting. Assuming that the appropriate people have been chosen to represent your firm, and assuming those representatives are well prepared, and assuming the situational factors have been manipulated in your favor, things can still go sour at the negotiation table. Obviously, if these other preliminaries haven't been managed properly, things *will* go wrong during the meetings. But even with great care and attention given to preliminary details, managing the dynamics of the negotiation process is almost always the greatest challenge facing Americans seeking to do business with the Japanese.

Negotiations on both sides of the Pacific proceed in four steps: (1) nontask sounding, (2) task-related exchange of information, (3) persuasion, and (4) concessions and agreement.

Nontask Sounding

The early stages of a business meeting usually include some talk not directly related to the topic at hand. Golf, weather, families, long airline flights, and the like, are often discussed before someone brings up business. We learn about the other people during such talk—their personalities, communication styles, backgrounds, and how they feel that day. All this information is valuable and necessary to know how to handle the rest of the meeting. In Japan, if this part of negotiations isn't managed properly, then the Japanese simply won't get down to business.

In Japan, top executives are included in business negotiations primarily as ceremonial figures. Their primary role is nontask sounding and they are seldom involved in the other stages. They are brought into the meetings early on to set a tone of cooperation or later to sign the final agreement. The nontask sounding can include much formality, ceremony, and time. Two or three meetings at offices, restaurants, and hotels is the norm. In all situations, task-related matters are not discussed; they are left to lower level managers. Top executives should prepare for such meetings by having a list of possible topics—activities of mutual friends, sports, general business climate, and so on. Reference to the Japanese executives' "Who's Who" will provide background for such discussions. Small gifts are appropriate. When such meetings are located in the United States we recommend a similar sort of Japanese formality.

At lower levels of management, nontask sounding will also take longer. The typical routine in Japan is to call on a client in the afternoon (with *shokai-sha*) to meet all the Japanese managers concerned and to chat about nontask matters. The afternoon meeting is usually followed by dinner and then by drinks in a nightclub. Throughout these activities, details of the prospective business are not discussed. The Japanese are not so much listening to what you say as how you say it. They are trying to get to know you. Until they feel comfortable they will not want to discuss business. So what often takes five to ten minutes, or at most a luncheon, in the United States can take all afternoon and evening and often longer in Japan. We strongly recommend you wait for your clients to bring up the business. This Japanese style of nontask sounding will certainly test your patience, but negotiations will go more efficiently if they trust you and a harmonious personal relationship has been established before business begins.

Task-Related Exchange of Information

An exchange of information implies both give and take. Most American negotiators report having to give a great deal to Japanese clients while receiving little in return.

Giving information to your Japanese clients and partners will require extra effort. Some of them will understand English, but in many cases an interpreter will still be required. Interpreters are readily available, but you should choose carefully a specialist in your area. Generally, you get what you pay for. We suggest you organize proposals and presentations differently—explanations first, then the requests. Be prepared for unusually detailed questions and questions from several different people. Also, be prepared to field the same question more than once. This is the Japanese style of making sure they understand your needs and preferences. This questioning can be carried too far, even in Japan, and you should be prepared to shorten your answers to repeated questions. We also suggest that you initially ask for more (higher price, faster delivery, etc.) in Japan than you might in the United States. This is their style and they expect you to leave yourself room to maneuver rather than making your best offer first. It will be important to guard against making concessions during this long questioning process. This is where your impatience can cause real problems. Finally, you should realize that from the Japanese point of view, the task-related exchange of information is the heart of a business negotiation. Be patient and expect to spend the most time at this stage.

If the Japanese are making the proposal, getting information will not be a problem. You will be wondering when they will get to the point, for they spend the most time with explanations before the actual requests. However, if your company is courting the Japanese business you should anticipate problems in getting feedback regarding your proposals. Their "Oh, it looks fine" often really means "it stinks." For several reasons the Japanese will be loathe to say no. In order to get true feelings from the Japanese side you must have established an informal, lower level channel of communication. Without such a source of information, you will truly be in the dark, for at the negotiation table, when everyone is present, only kind, face-saving responses to your questions will be heard. Because this informal channel of communication is so important, if you're having difficulty establishing it we recommend you ask *shokai-sha* to help. Finally, you should take careful notes of the meetings, including a tally of the questions they ask. Much can be deduced about Japanese bargainers' true interests by analyzing their questions.

Persuasion

In Japan there is not a clear separation of the task-related exchange of information and persuasion. The two stages tend to blend together as each side more clearly defines and refines its needs and preferences. So much time is spent at this task-related exchange of information that little is left to argue about during the persuasion stage.

However, from the American perspective once we know what each side wants, then the challenge of trying to bring the other side closer to our proposal begins. In America we have a wide range of persuasive tactics that can be and often are employed to change our clients' minds.

The choice of persuasive tactics in Japan is very much constrained by status relations and the appropriate communication channel. That is, sellers never use aggressive persuasive tactics. Buyers only use them indirectly, through the lower level, informal communication channel. Therefore, in your dealings with Japanese executives we recommend using the following persuasive tactics in the following order:

1. Ask more questions. This is the single most important persuasive tactic in Japan and in the United States. If they don't have good answers, they will make concessions.

2. Explain again your company's situations, needs, and preferences.

3. Use other positive influence tactics—promises, recommendations, rewards, and positive normative appeals.

4. If you're still not satisfied with their response, try silence. Let them think about it and give them an opportunity to change their position.

5. If tactics 1 through 4 don't work, then it's time to change the subject or call a recess and use the informal communication channel. But rather than going directly to the more aggressive tactics we recommend repeating tactics 1 through 4. The questions and explanations may elicit new information or objectives that could not be broached at the negotiation table.

6. Aggressive influence tactics may be used in negotiations with Japanese at great risk and in special circumstances. First, they should only be used via the informal channel, and even then only in the most indirect manner possible. Rather than saying, "If your company can't lower its price, then we'll go to another supplier," it would be better to say, "Lower prices on the part of your company would go a long way toward our not having to consider other options available to us." Second, they should be used only when the American company is clearly in the stronger position. Even in these two circumstances, use of such aggres-

sive persuasive tactics will damage the *wa*, which may in the long run be to your company's disadvantage. If power relations ever shift, the Japanese will be quick to exploit the change in events. However, if the American side exercised restraint and maintains the *wa*, then if and when power relations shift, the Japanese side will consider the American company's interests.

7. If tactics 1 through 6 have not produced Japanese concessions, next we suggest the use of time. Give them time to consider new information and time to reach a consensus. The Japanese will rarely make concessions immediately following your persuasive appeals because the entire group must be consulted and agree. This takes time.

8. The next persuasive tactic to use is asking the *chukai-sha* or *shokai-sha* to arbitrate your differences. Let them call your clients and meet as a go-between. We have seen *chukai-sha* successfully settle otherwise irreconcilable differences. However, serious consideration should be given to making concessions yourself before calling in *chukai-sha*. Third-party mediation will ordinarily work only once.

9. Finally, as a last resort, it may be worthwhile to bring together the top executives of your companies in the hopes of stimulating more cooperation using a top-down approach. However, such a tactic is fraught with danger, particularly if negative influence tactics have been used in the past. A refusal at this stage means the business is finished.

To conclude our discussion of persuasive tactics, we want to emphasize the importance of our recommendations. A mistake at this stage, even a minor one, can have large consequences on your Japanese business. American managers will have to be doubly conscientious to avoid blunders here because the Japanese style of persuasion is so different and apparently cumbersome. Remember that the Japanese are looking to establish a long-term business relationship for mutual benefit. Threats don't fit into their understanding of how such a relationship should work. They are not in a hurry; they are concerned about *wa* and cooperation in the long run. You should also recognize that we are recommending adoption of a Japanese approach to persuasion when bargaining with Japanese clients and business partners. We realize it takes longer, but in the end you and your company will benefit by such an approach. Finally, smart American negotiators will anticipate the Japanese use of the same nine persuasive tactics.

Concessions and Agreement

The final stage of business negotiations involves concessions, building toward agreement. Negotiations require compromise. Usually, both sides give up something to get even more. But the approach used for compromise differs on each side of the Pacific. In America we tend to use a sequential approach—considering and settling one issue at a time. Progress is easily measured. We're half way through when we're through half the issues. However, in Japan all issues are examined simultaneously in a more holistic approach. Concessions are made only near the end of the talks and usually all at once. Thus, Americans bargaining with Japanese often think little progress is being made.

The signs of progress in Japanese-American discussions are different. Positive signals are (1) focusing questions on specific topics, (2) including more senior executives in the talks, (3) softening a position, and (4) increasing the use of informal channels of communication.

Finally, be certain to follow your plan for concession making, put together before the talks begin. Also, make concessions only after breaks during which you have taken an opportunity to think things out away from the social pressure of the meeting.

Minor Distractions

Japanese meeting etiquette is different from Americans'. Don't be alarmed if they have side conversations in Japanese, leave in the middle of meetings, or listen with their eyes closed.

AFTER NEGOTIATIONS
(Chapter 7)

Once verbal agreements have been reached, it is time to consider what follows the negotiations.

Contracts

In the United States executives talk of "concluding business deals." In Japan executives speak about "establishing business relationships." These basic attitudes strongly influence the form of contracts in the two countries. The American style contract tends to be long and includes numerous carefully worded clauses regarding every aspect of the agreement and anticipating every contingency. Alternatively, Japanese contracts are very short and descriptive. The Japanese depend on good personal and business relationships to handle the inevitable contingencies, not lawyers and lawsuits. These differing forms of contracts will require negotiation and compromise. We recommend that you push for the kind of contract with which you and your counsel feel comfortable. But you should anticipate long delays if a Japanese lawyer is required. They are more meticulous than you can imagine.

More worldly Japanese partners and clients will understand your need for an American style contract. Indeed, they may even prefer one if they've been "burned" by Americans in the past. But executives of smaller companies, inexperienced in transactions with Americans may become suspicious of your intentions. In this latter circumstance you will have to explain to your clients your need for the contract.

Signing Ceremonies

Ceremony is a required part of signing agreements with your Japanese business partners. Be patient and put your culture aside on this one. Remember, Americans are the odd ones in the world when it comes to formality.

Headquarters' Assessment of the Agreement

Avoid having to renege on your agreements by maintaining good communications with your home office. If you misrepresent your firm's interests and are forced to renege, your dealings with the Japanese are over. Your company may be able to salvage something, but the Japanese won't talk to you personally again.

Japanese headquarters' assessments of business agreements are uniformly positive. Everyone knows the details and everyone agrees—a consensus was reached. Therefore, implementation of the agreement will be fast. Also, subsequent negotiations on other issues will go faster because the all-important personal relationships have been established. This suggests a strategy for American companies. Establish relationships during easy negotiations. Save the tough, more complex deals for later.

Follow-Up Communications

Just as personal considerations are more important during negotiations with Japanese clients, they are also important after the negotiations are concluded. Obviously, you will be in touch with your Japanese clients and partners regarding the business of the relationship. But it will be equally important to keep personal relationships warm. Expect frequent visits form the Japanese. Write personal notes to all the Japanese participants. Your top executive should send a formal note to their top executive. Periodic personal notes with pictures or articles of interest are also a good idea. Finally, only with careful consideration and great reluctance should you switch your key personnel involved with your Japanese clients. Switching will require a new round of nontask sounding and *wa* building.

Adjustments to Agreements

Include an arbitration clause in your agreement, but avoid using it at all costs. We recommend conferral first, *chukai-sha* second, and arbitration last. Even if you "win," the business relationship will never be the same if an arbitrator is required.

11 PRESCRIPTIONS FOR JAPANESE TRAVELING IN THE UNITED STATES

In this chapter we present our ideas on how Japanese executives should adapt their behavior and expectations when negotiating with American clients or partners. We hope that this chapter will give you an even better understanding of business negotiations American style.

AN INTERVIEW WITH HIRONARI MASAGO

Hironari Masago is a former director general of MITI, and is presently serving as the senior executive director for the Osaka Chamber of Commerce. He is a lawyer by training and spent one year at the Harvard Law School to enhance his Japanese legal training. He was involved in the first round of talks between MITI and the U.S. Trade Representative regarding automobile export quotas and was in large part responsible for the agreements that have served to dampen an otherwise volatile trade issue. Masago also served as *shokai-sha* and as an adviser for several Japanese companies interested in American investments or partnerships.

We talked with Masago at the Kahala Hilton in Honolulu as he relaxed after a difficult negotiation. A large Japanese firm was looking to acquire a smaller American firm. The negotiation was not going particularly well, and Masago attributed part of the problem to differences in the style of Japanese and American negotiators. He related to us some of his own experiences and his advice for Japanese dealing with Americans.

> Preparations for negotiations are critical. Two years ago I acted as an adviser to JUSCO [a large Japanese food retailer] in their talks with General Mills regarding a joint venture to open a chain of Red Lobster Restaurants in Japan. We carefully gathered from secondary sources all financial and personal information about General Mills and the firm's top executives. But most importantly, I consulted with my school chum, Den Fujita, head of McDonald's in Japan. He provided specific information about the American food service industry and suggested the structure of the deal we should bargain for. In particular Fujita-san felt a fifty-fifty joint venture with a substantial financial commitment from the Americans was best. He also stressed the importance of having an all-Japanese board directing the joint venture. That is, General Mills should have a number of its own Japanese executives serve with the JUSCO board members. Through our extensive preparations, using both secondary sources of public information, and the valuable advice of Den Fujita, we were able to put together the joint venture agreement successfully.

Masago also suggests that Japanese business negotiators heed the following recommendations:

1. Always ask for an American style contract, but with jurisdiction in Japan. The American commercial legal system is incredibly complex, with differences in each state.

2. Establish a trusting relationship. It will take longer with American clients, but don't talk business until you feel completely comfortable.

3. Don't use a "banana sale" approach with the Americans. Such high initial demands will sour relationships with American bargainers. They will not understand.

4. Be prepared for the "Texas approach"—threats and aggressive tactics. Watch out for bluffs, but recognize the need to compromise if the threats are real. Be ready with alternative plans to use in the face of such threats. (We feel that Masago's choice of words, "the Texas approach," is very revealing of the Japanese view of the American stereotypical "John Wayne style.")

5. Don't lose your ability to negotiate. It is your job to persuade and do not just act as a go-between. Make sure you have the

responsibility and authority to represent your company. If you don't, or if the Americans perceive that you don't, the Americans will be unwilling to make compromises at the negotiation table.

6. *Nemawashi* will be very important.

7. Having an informal channel for communication and negotiation is critical.

8. Finally, in the end, he who has more information will win. This is the key. But you should also understand that if both sides are well informed, then both sides can win.

SELECTION OF NEGOTIATORS IN JAPAN

Selection of the most appropriate bargainers will be important for dealings with Americans. Japanese negotiators should be:

1. Outgoing—unafraid to start a conversation with foreigners and ask questions;

2. Adaptable (or flexible)—comfortable in new and unusual environments and willing to learn;

3. Fluent in English—should comprehend the subtle nuances of the American's use of English including the use of sarcasm, irony, figures of speech, and so on;

4. Creative—willing to suggest and consider new alternatives;

5. Knowledgeable about the importance of American style contracts;

6. Exhibit high aspirations—important for the success of the negotiation and the mutual benefits for the business partners;

7. Self-motivated—assumes responsibility for the conduct of the negotiations; and

8. Experienced in negotiations with American clients. Such experiences begin with lower level assignments, as note takers and listeners. On-the-job experience is considered the best negotiation training.

NEGOTIATION PRELIMINARIES

Be as well prepared as possible for your negotiations with the Americans. Carefully manipulate the negotiation setting to your advantage.

Efficient Preparations

In the United States there will be even more information available on publicly held firms than in Japan. We also strongly recommend the counsel of an associate who has dealt with the American firm previously. Realize that your American clients will not only have a list of topics and issues to discuss but also a specific order of discussion in mind. Your deviations from their order may disrupt the talks.

Manipulation of the Negotiation Setting

Invite the Americans to bargain in Japan or at least in a neutral site like Hawaii. The Americans will tend to favor informality and display a disregard for normal business etiquette—politeness, seating arrangements, and so on. Don't read subtle messages into their nonchalance; it is their way of feeling comfortable. The Americans will generally bring small negotiation teams, often only one person. They will not understand the differing roles and responsibilities of operational staff, middle managers, and top executives. You should maintain your usual contingent of negotiators as it affords a subtle power that you can exploit. Americans in their apparent rush to get things done will often try to get all parties in a deal together and attempt to hammer out an agreement. They do not understand the importance of *nemawashi*. Americans like to use the telephone and telex to an amazing degree and for unusual purposes like nontask sounding. Finally, you will notice Americans' impatience and imposition of time limits. They will also try to impose time constraints, and in response you should carefully explain *ringi-sho*. You should anticipate these differences in style and manipulate the negotiation setting to suit your purposes.

AT THE NEGOTIATION TABLE

Nontask Sounding

Americans do not understand the importance of trusting personal relationships. They depend on their lawyers to write tight contracts and settle disputes. Thus, they tend to skip over nontask sounding. We recommend that you explain to them the importance of this first stage of business negotiations and that you proceed to economics only when you feel comfortable.

Task-Related Exchange of Information

Ask questions and expect frank, even blunt answers. The Americans will also give you short answers and get impatient at requests for more detail. In the United States negotiators are anxious to get through the exchange of information so that the "real" negotiation—persuasion—can begin. We recommend you ask your questions anyway. Finally, the American style of presentation of a proposal is backwards. They say what they want and then explain why. Moreover, they will often not bother with explanations unless you request them.

Don't use banana sale first offers. Time and again we have seen carefully developed harmonious relationships destroyed by Japanese banana sale first offers. Don't expect Americans to read your subtle, nonverbal responses. Try to be frank and state clearly your company's needs and preferences. Americans are deaf to *hara-gei* and other subtle messages. You may also have to take the initiative in establishing the informal communication channel, and they may view use of such a medium as unethical. We recommend you have *shokai-sha* explain the rules about informal communication channels to your prospective American partners. In making your presentations to Americans you may want to make your offer first, and then provide the explanation.

Persuasion

From the American point of view this is the heart of the negotiation. You should anticipate the "Texas style" aggressive arguments, even threats. Threats and warnings from American bargainers don't have the same meaning as they do in Japan. Americans don't understand the art of indirectness and the importance of informal communication channels or *shokai-sha* for such heavy persuasive tactics. Even more incredible is their ignorance of how status relationships determine how and what can be said. Indeed, both American buyers and sellers use the same aggressive persuasive tactics.

Your most powerful persuasive tactics will be your questions, silences, and delays. All these tactics will elicit concessions from Americans. Their outstanding cultural characteristic is impatience, and they view concessions as a way to move things along more quickly.

Concessions and Agreement

We recommend sticking to a more holistic discussion of the several negotiation issues. Americans will try to take a sequential approach, settling one issue before discussing and settling the second, third, and fourth. However, use the Japanese style. You should be aware, however, that your American partners will be unable to read progress in the talks. This may hurt or help you, and you should carefully monitor and manage their frustration resulting from an approach they consider haphazard.

Americans will also make concessions at the negotiation table, without consultation. The American management system is top-down, and the senior negotiator will make concessions despite the objections of his advisors. Your consensus decisionmaking style is a good safeguard against such "snap" decisions.

AFTER NEGOTIATIONS

After American negotiators make agreements, they must often then sell the agreement to their headquarters. And usually the headquarters' assessment of the agreement is less favorable than you might expect. This may cause delays in the implementation of their side of the agreement. In very unusual circumstances, they may even renege. In the latter situation we suggest you bypass the representative and bargain directly with the real decisionmakers.

We strongly recommend American style written contracts with Japanese jurisdiction. Because American personnel change frequently, the written contract is your only assurance of compliance with the agreement. We also recommend an arbitration clause—Japan Commercial Arbitration Association or a third-country arbitrator such as the International Chamber of Commerce Court of Arbitration. Of course, we suggest you try to resolve conflicts with your American partners through conferral. But you should recognize that they do not share your strong aversion to arbitration.

Finally, Americans generally don't share your views about keeping personal relationships warm. Ordinarily, they will contact you only about commercial matters, and they will be surprised, even suspicious, with your frequent nontask visits and communications. Also, they will not understand the importance of an official signing ceremony, so you must explain.

America is a most heterogenous culture. Not everyone acts like John Wayne. Indeed, consider the difference in negotiation styles of Alexander Haig and George Schultz. And understand that the roles of minorities and women are changing fast in the United States. You should anitcipate key negotiation roles being filled by women and minority executives. They should not be treated any differently than the Caucasian male executives with whom you are more accustomed to dealing.

APPENDIX
Directory of Selected Organizations and Information Centers

EMBASSY OF JAPAN, JAPANESE CONSULATES AND THEIR JURISDICTIONAL AREAS IN THE UNITED STATES

Japanese Embassy and Consulates are official representatives of Japan in the United States. In addition to visa-issuing services, they are equipped to answer business questions. Economic consuls sent by the Ministry of Finance or the Ministry of International Trade and Industry often respond to your inquiries and questions. Most of the consulate offices have a library of government official publications and selected reference books.

— Embassy of Japan, 2520 Massachusetts Avenue, N.W., Washington, D.C., 20008-2869, 202-234-2266.

Consulates of Japan:

— 909 West 9th Avenue, Suite 301, Anchorage, Alaska 99501, 907-279-8428.

— 400 Colony Square Bldg., Suite 1501, 1201 Peachtree Street, N.E., Atlanta, Georgia 30361, 404-892-2700.

151

- 625 North Michigan Avenue, Chicago, Illinois 60611, 312-280-0400.
- 1742 Nuuanu Avenue, Honolulu, Hawaii 96817-3294, 808-536-2226.
- 1612 First City National Bank Bld., 1021 Main Street, Houston, Texas 77002, 713-652-2977/9.
- 250 East First Street, Suite 1507, Los Angeles, California 90012, 213-624-8305.
- 280 Park Avenue, New York, New York 10017, 212-986-1600.
- 1830 International Trade Mart Bldg., No. 2 Canal Street, New Orleans, Louisiana 70130, 504-529-2101/2.
- 2400 First Interstate Tower, 1300 S.W. 5th Avenue, Portland, Oregon 92701, 503-221-1811.
- 1601 Post Street, San Francisco, California 94115, 415-921-8000.
- 3110 Rainier Bank Tower, 1301 Fifth Avenue, Seattle, Washington 98101, 206-682-9107.
- 2519 Commerce Tower, 911 Main Street, Kansas City, Missouri 64105-2076, 816-471-0111.
- Federal Reserve Plaza, 14th Floor, 600 Atlantic Avenue, Boston, Massachusetts 02210, 617-973-9772.

JAPANESE CONSULATES AND THEIR JURISDICTIONAL AREAS IN CANADA

- Embassy of Japan, 255 Sussex Drive, Ottawa, Ontario, 1-613-233-6214.

Consulates of Japan:

- Toronto Dominion Centre, Suite 1803, P.O. Box 10, Toronto, Ontario, 416-363-7038.
- 1155 Dorchester West Blvd., Suite 2701, Montreal, Quebec, H3B-2K9, 514-866-3429.
- 730-215 Garry Street, Credit Union Central Plaza, Winnipeg, Manitoba, R3C 3P3, 204-943-5554.
- 10020-100th Street, Suite 2600, Edmonton, Alberta, T5J ON4, 403-422-3752, 403-429-3052.
- 1210-1177 West Hastings Street, Vancouver, B.C., J6E 2K9, 604-684-5868.

JAPAN TRADE CENTER (JAPAN EXTERNAL TRADE ORGANIZATION) IN NORTH AMERICA

The Japan External Trade Organization (JETRO): A semi-governmental, nonprofit organization, JETRO conducts public relations promotion abroad as well as research on international economic trade and trends. Japan Trade Centers are its overseas agencies. JETRO has been actively assisting American enterprises in their efforts to export their products to Japan. It has established a "Business Consultation System" which introduces new products for possible exportation into the Japanese market. Through this system, the product is evaluated under Japanese consumer standards by experts from Japanese trading companies and department stores. They are staffed with business consultants and maintain an extensive reference library.

Japan Trade Center, New York 44th floor, McGraw-Hill bldg., 1221 Avenue of the Americas, New York, N.Y. 10020-1060, U.S.A. 212-997-0400.

Japan Trade Center, Chicago 230 North Michigan Avenue, Chicago, Illinois 60601, U.S.A. 312-726-4390 to 4392, 4779.

Japan Trade Center, Houston 1221 McKenney, One Houston Center, Suite 1810, Houston, Texas 77010, U.S.A. 713-759-9595, 9596, 9597.

Japan Trade Center, Los Angeles 555 South Flower Street, Los Angeles, California, 90071, U.S.A. 213-626-5700.

Japan Trade Center, San Francisco Suite 501, 5th Floor, Qantas Building, 360 Post Street, San Francisco, CA 94108, U.S.A. 415-392-1333.

Japan Trade Center, Toronto Suite 700 Britannica House, 151 Bloor Street West, Toronto, Ontario, CANADA, M5S 1T7. 416-962-5050.

Japan Trade Center, Room 812, Royal Bank Building, 10117 Jasper Avenue, Edmonton, Alberta T5J IW8. 403-428-0866.

Japan Trade Center, Montreal 50 Frontenac, Floor F, Place Bonaventure, Montreal 114, P.Q. Canada. 514-861-5240, 861-4554.

Japan Trade Center, Vancouver Room No. 916, Standard Bldg., 510 West Hasting Street, Vancouver, B.C., Canada V6B IL8. 604-684-4174.

United States–Japan Trade Council, Inc.: 100 Connecticut Avenue N.W., Washington, D.C. 20036. 202-296-5633.

A DIRECTORY OF RESOURCES IN JAPAN

Embassy of Canada, 3–38 Akasaka 7-chome, Minato-ku, Tokyo. 03–408–2101.

Embassy of the U.S.A., 2, Aoi-cho, Minato-ku, Tokyo. 03–583–7141.

Business Information Center, c/o Embassy of the U.S.A. 1F. 03–583–7141, Ext. 7549. (The Business Information Center in the American Embassy has a number of staff members who can provide guidance for conducting business in Japan. They have an extensive library and publish the *Japan Market Information Report*. This center also acts as the information resource for those Japanese businessmen wishing to do business with the Americans.)

U.S. Consulates

Osaka: Sankei Bldg., 27, Umeda-cho, Kita-ku. 06–34102754.

Fukuoka: 5–26, Ohori 2-chome, Chuo-ku. 092–751–9331.

Sapporo: 1, Nishi 13-chome, Kita 1–jo, Chuo-Ku. 011–221–5121.

Kobe: 10, Kano-cho 6–chome, Ikuta-ku. 978–331–9679.

Naha: 2129, Gusukuma, Urasoe, Okinawa. 0988–778142, 0988–778627.

American Center Library (The American Center Library is the English language library for Americans in Japan)

Tokyo: ABC Bldg., 20603, Shiba Koen, Minato-ku. 436–0901.

Osaka: Sankei Bldg., 27, Umeda-cho, Kita-ku. 345–0601.

Kyoto: 657, Higashi Monzen-cho, Sokokuji, Kamigyo-ku. 241–1211.

Nagoya: Yokota Bldg., 2028–24, Izumi, Higashi-ku. 931–8907.

Fukuoka: 1–3–36, Tenjin, Chuo-ku. 761–6667.

Sapporo: Hishi 12, Kita 2, Chuo-ku. 251–9211.

Other Information Centers

American Chamber of Commerce of Japan (ACCJ), 701 Tosho Bldg., 14–3 Marunouchi, Chiyoda-ku, Tokyo. (ACCJ is the chamber of those American companies established and operated in Japan. Listening to the opinions, experiences and knowledge of their members may be quite valuable to your negotiations. They may help you select counsel, consultants, or accountants.)

The Federation of Bankers Association of Japan, 3-1 Marunouchi 1-chome, Chiyoda-ku, Tokyo. 03-216-3761 (For information about Japanese banks.)

Federation of Economic Organizations (Keidanren), Keidanren Kaikan, 9-4, Otemachi 1-chome, Chiyoda-ku, Tokyo. 01-279-1411 (Keidanren is THE organization of the business organizations in Japan. They compile a great amount of financial and commercial information.)

Government Publication Service Center, 2, Kasumigaseki 1-chome, Chiyoda-ku, Tokyo, JAPAN. 03-504-2581.

The Japan Chamber of Commerce & Industry, 2-2, Marunouchi 3-chome, Chiyoda-ku, Tokyo 100. 03-283-7500.

Japan External Trade Organization (JETRO Tokyo), 2-5, Toranomon 2-chome, Minato-ku, Tokyo 105. 03-582-5511.

  Over the Counter Service, International Information Service, Japan External Trade Organization.

  International Lounge, International Communication Department, Japan External Trade Organization.

JETRO Osaka, Bingomachi Bldg., 2051, Bingomachi, Higashi-ku, Osaka 541. 06-203-3601.

JETRO Nagoya Office, Aichiken Sangyo Boekikan Nishikan, 407, Marunouchi 2-chome, Naka-ku, Nagoya 460. 052-211-4517.

Japan Federation of Employers' Association (Nikkeiren) 406, Marunouchi 1-chome, Chiyoda-ku Tokyo Tel: 03-213-4451.

Japan Tariff Association, No. 2 Jibiki Bldg., 7-8, Kojimachi 4-chome, Chiyoda-ku, Tokyo. 03-263-7221.

Manufactured Imports Promotion Organization, World Import Mart Bldg., 6F., P.O. Box 2129, 1-3, Higashi-ikebukuro 3-chome, Toshima-ku, Tokyo 170. 03-988-2791.

The Japan Federation of Importers Organization, Daiwa Bldg., 6-1, Nihonbashi Honcho 1-chome, Chuo-ku, Tokyo 103. 03-270-0791.

Japan Department Stores Association, Yanagiya Bldg., 1-10, Nihonbashi 2-chome, Chuo-ku, Tokyo 103. 03-272-1666.

Japan Chain Stores Association, Toranomon No. 40 Mori Bldg. 6F., 13-1 Toranomon 5-chome, Minato-ku, Tokyo 105. 03-433-1290.

Keizai Koho Center (Japan Institute for Social and Economic Affairs) 61-, Otemachi 1-chome, Chiyoda-ku, Tokyo, JAPAN 100. 03-201-1415. (Keizai Koho Center is a private nonprofit organization that works in cooperation with Keidanren— Japan Federation of Economic Organizations.)

Business Information Centers Provided by Major Hotels in Japan

Executive Service Salon (ESS).   Hotel Okura, 10–4, Toranomon 2-chome, Minato-ku, Tokyo 105, Japan. 03–582–0111 Ext. 3090.

Okura was the first to provide business center service in the Far East. Provides one of the best communication services among many Tokyo hotels with bilingual receptionists. Some of the services provided are:

— Arrangement for bilingual secretaries and consecutive and simultaneous interpreters
— Help research the project with Data Bank of Nihon Keizai Shimbun and Okura English Language Reference Library
— Equipment rental.

JAL's Executive Service Lounge.   Imperial Hotel 101, 1-chome, Uchisaiwaicho, Chiyoda-ku, Tokyo, Japan. 03–504–1111.

Services provided:

— Business Information Service
— Appointment set up
— Secretarial and interpretation arrangements.

Executive Business Center.   Akasaka Prince Hotel 1–2, Kioi-cho, Chiyoda-ku, Tokyo 102, Japan. 03–234–111 Ext. 5278.

Services provided:

— Information services
— Office services, including Tokyo area messenger services
— Multilingual interpreting and translation
— Business consulting
— Equipment rental.

Other hotels that provide business information center services.

The New Otani Club.   The New Otani Hotel & Tower, 4, Kioi-Cho, Chiyoda-ku, Tokyo, JAPAN 102. 03–265–1111.

Palace Hotel, 1–1, 1-chome, Marunouchi, Chiyoda-ku, Tokyo.

Other Important Directories:

The Economic and Industrial Organization in Japan, Revised August 1, 1982, The Tokyo Chamber of Commerce and Industry.

Japan Company Handbook, Published biannually, Toyo Keizai Shimposha, 1-4, Motoizumi-cho, Nihonbashi Chuo-ku, Tokyo T103.

Japan Economic Yearbook, Published by The Oriental Economist Ltd., 4, Hongoku-cho, 1-chome, Nihonbashi, Chuo-ku, Tokyo. 03-270-4111.

The Japan Times Directory of Foreign Residents, Business Firms and Organizations, Published by The Japan Times, Ltd., 5-4, Shibaura 4-chome, Minato-ku, Tokyo, T108.

Japan Trade Directory 1983, Japan External Trade Organization (JETRO) Publication Department, 205, Toranomon, 2-chome, Minato-ku, Tokyo.

Standard Trade Index of Japan 1983-84, compiled and published by The Japan Chamber of Commerce and Industry, Suite 505, World Trade Center Bldg., 4-1, Hamamatsu-Cho 2-chome, Minato-ku, Tokyo, T105.

Yellow Pages Japan Telephone Book, Published by Japan Yellow Pages, Ltd., ST Bldg., 609 Iidabashi, 4-chome, Chiyoda-ku, Tokyo, T102. 03-239-3501.

Japan Company Directory, Published by The Oriental Economist Ltd., 4, Hongoku-cho, 1-chome, Nihonbashi Chuo-ku, Tokyo.

The President Directory, Published by Diamond Time Co., Ltd., 4-2, Kasumigaseki 1-chome, Chiyoda-ku, Tokyo. 03-504-6600.

Japan Business Directory, Published by Diamond Lead Co., Ltd., 4-2, Kasumigaseki 1-chome, Chiyoda-ku, Tokyo.

JIT (Japan Industrial Trade Index), Published by JIT International Inc., 21-10, Kanda Misakicho 2-chome, Chiyoda-ku, Tokyo.

Japanese Institutes

Mitsubishi Economic Research Institute
3-1, Marunouchi 3-chome, Chiyoda-ku, Tokyo. 03-214-4416.

The Japan Economic Research Center
Nikkei Bldg., 9-5, Otemachi, 1-chome, Chiyoda-ku, Tokyo. 03-270-5541.

Nomura Research Institute of Technology and Economics
6, Nihonbashi-Edobashi 1-chome, Chuo-ku, Tokyo. 03-211-3811.

Nikko Research Center
Shin Tokyo Bldg., 3-1, Marunouchi 3-chome, Chiyoda-ku, Tokyo. 03-212-7531.

Institute of International Investment
23-10, Matsubara 5-chome, Minato-ku, Tokyo. 03-321-0080.

World Economic Information Services
World Trade Center Bldg., 4–1, Hamamatsucho 2-chome, Minato-ku, Tokyo. 03–435–5740.

Japan Securities Research Institute
Tokyo Shoken Kaikan, 14, Kayaba-cho 1-chome, Nihonbashi, Chuo-ku, Tokyo. 03–669–0737.

GLOSSARY OF JAPANESE
BUSINESS TERMS

aisatsu: a formal greeting.

amae: indulgent dependency.

banana no tataki uri: the "banana sale" approach.

bucho: general manager.

chukai-sha: mediators.

hara: abdomen or stomach ("gut").

hara-gei: negotiation between executives without the use of direct words.

honne: true mind, real intention.

ishin-denshin: nonverbal communication.

kabanmochi: assistants.

kacho: section chief.

kikkake: an opening, an opportunity.

kosai-hi: entertainment expense.

nagai tsukiai: long-term relationship.

naniwabushi: a seller's approach.

nemawashi: preparing the roots (lobbying).

onsha: your great company.

otaku: your company.

ringi-kessai: decisionmaking by consensus.

ringi-sho: document used for consensus decisionmaking.

seme: account of critical events.
shacho: chief executive officer.
Shinshiroku: Japanese "Who's Who."
shinyo: gut feeling, "trust in the viscera."
shokai-sha: introducers.
sutaffu: operational staff level.
tatemae: truthful, official stance.
tate shakai: living and working in a vertical society.
urei: pathos and sorrow.
wa: interpersonal harmony.

INDEX

161

ABOUT THE AUTHORS

John L. Graham is assistant professor of marketing at the University of Southern California Graduate School of Business and research associate in USC's International Business Education and Research Program. He received a Ph.D. in business administration at the University of California, Berkeley, and has served as a marketing analyst for Solar Turbines, Inc., a division of Caterpillar Tractors. Graham's articles on international negotiations have appeared in several academic and management journals, including the *Harvard Business Review* and the *Columbia Journal of World Business.*

Yoshihiro Sano is a native of Japan and was educated there prior to obtaining degrees in economics, business administration, and international business from the University of California, Los Angeles and the University of Southern California. Before his present position as a business consultant for Ernst & Whinney, Yoshi was associate director of the International Business Education and Research Program at the University of Southern California.